POWER
In No Other Name

Overcome Life's Problems God's *Way*

A spiritual journey of truth, hope and freedom

By
Grand Master Dong Jin Kim
and
Reverend Steve Hannett

RAGGED EDGE PRESS
SHIPPENSBURG, PENNSYLVANIA

This Ragged Edge Press publication
was printed by
Beidel Printing House, Inc.
63 West Burd Street
Shippensburg, PA 17257-0708 USA

The acid-free paper used in this book meets the guidelines for permanence and durability of the Committee on Production Guidelines for Book Longevity of the Council on Library Resources.

For a complete list of available publications
please write
Ragged Edge Press
Division of White Mane Publishing Company, Inc.
P.O. Box 708
Shippensburg, PA 17257-0708 USA

Library of Congress Cataloging-in-Publication Data

Kim, Dong Jin, 1956-
    Power in no other name : overcome life's problems God's way : a spiritual journey of truth, hope, and freedom / by Dong Jin Kim & Steve Hannett.
        p. cm.
    ISBN 1-57249-333-X (alk. paper)
    1. Christian life. 2. Suffering--Religious aspects--Christianity. I. Hannett, Steve, 1974- II. Title.

BV4501.3 .K55 2002
248.8'6--dc21

                                                            2002031826

PRINTED IN THE UNITED STATES OF AMERICA

This book is written in thanks and praise to the Lord Jesus Christ for His love and faithfulness toward all people who want to know Him

and

To all those seeking relief and healing from sickness, disease, weakness, and oppression of all kinds. May you be blessed by the power and promises of God the Father through His Son, Jesus Christ, Savior of the world.

Special Thanks and Appreciation to:
Pastor Paul Beh
Carl Figueroa
Kate Hannett

Contents

People overcame these problems! Learn how!

Allergies
Anxiety attacks
Arthritis
Asthma
Breast cancer
Bone spurs
Bursitis
Cancer
Canker sores
Carpal tunnel
Chronic back pain
Common cold
Diabetes
Digestive problems
Drug addiction
Encephalitis photogenic amnesia
Enlarged heart
Insomnia
Knee injuries
Epstein-Barr virus
Fevers
Gout
Headache

Hearing problems
Hypoglycemia
Mastopathy
Mental problems
Migraines
Motion sickness
Muscle injuries
Optic neuritis
Panic attacks
Pinched nerves
Salmonella poisoning
Seizure disorder
Spinal degenerative disease
Sinus Inflammation
Skin disorders
Skin rashes
Stomach virus
Stroke damage
Tendonitis
Tonsillitis
Tumors
Warts
Wrist & ankle injuries

Foreword

I lift up the name of the Lord for He has kept His promise to raise up a corps of "Elijahs" in the end times. Jesus answered and said to them, *"Indeed, Elijah is coming first and will restore all things. But I say to you that Elijah has come already, and they did not know him, but did to him whatever they wished..."* (Matthew 17:11–12) John the Baptist came to make the path straight for the Lord, yet he could not restore all things. This restoration of "all things" continues today in the perfecting of His Bride, the Church, in these end times.

Despite conventional and traditional shortcomings of theological study, the Lord has indeed raised up "Elijahs" to prepare His second coming, and has blessed His saints of all levels with signs and wonders through the Holy Spirit. I have for a long time preached that the time is here for the Lord to raise up many of the market-place apostles, and market-place prophets like Joseph, Daniel, and Amos. To include the ministry of Conquerors In Christ, led by Grand Master Dong Jin Kim and Reverend Steve Hannett, is a certainty. The work of Conquerors In Christ World Ministries has continued for nearly 20 years and has been a great blessing to many. Indeed those that have faith in His word continue to witness His coming Kingdom in the strongest and most powerful ways possible.

My wife and I have both personally witnessed and experienced the powerful truths communicated in this book. I suffered with bad allergies for over 50 years, and my wife suffered with chronic migraines for over 10 years. Her pain was so severe that no pain-killer, not even powerful prescriptions, could help. For 15 years I tried every method I could, but experienced no relief. I then came to realize that our problems were not from natural origin, but were the works of spiritual enemies described in the Bible.

Grand Master Kim ministered to us with hesitation for he supposed that I, an ordained minister, should do it myself. I seemed to understand why it was necessary for us to be ministered by him, yet I am obliged to keep it from being expressed. But I can say two things. The first one is a matter of humility, and the second is a matter of the flow of the anointing in the Lord's will. When Grand Master Kim prayed and commanded the enemies to leave us in the name of Jesus Christ, claiming that my wife and I were children of God, every malady left, and we were healed 100 percent! I thank God for the healing we received.

Grand Master Dong Jin Kim has not only received gifts through faith with which he has ministered to many, but has also been blessed with a revelatory, yet sound, deep biblical knowledge. In fact, his biblical understanding of the reality of the devil is so unique that I have not heard or read this kind of information prior to reading this book.

Although this book represents only a portion of what the Lord has revealed, it clearly and emphatically communicates the base knowledge necessary for you to overcome whatever trouble or difficulty you may be facing. You will absolutely learn the reality of the spiritual world through and in between the lines of this book. I pray that you may learn the essential and indispensable truth of how to resist the devil. *"Be sober, be vigilant; because your adversary the devil walks about like a roaring lion, seeking whom he may devour."* (Peter 5:8) Praise the Lord!

I commend Reverend Steve Hannett, a servant of the Lord, who is faithful and bold for the work of God, and was also healed from a deadly disease as a result of God's promises in the Bible. Through prayer and study, I have come to believe that it was one of the reasons for the Lord to bless Steve with a ministry with the same and more powerful anointing. He has become a friend and a partner in ministry. It is another wonderful example of making disciples for the Kingdom of God in the end times!

I pray that the Spirit of the Lord may bless all the readers of this book to receive a double portion of the gifts of the Holy Spirit. Amen.

REVEREND PAUL BEH
NEW JERSEY

Introduction

Consider our present world. Things seem to be progressing rather well. Family income and college attendance are increasing, technology is growing at record speed, and world commerce is booming. Despite these positive signs, a closer and more honest consideration reveals a world in a tailspin of disarray. Today in the 21st century, children kill other children. Hate crimes are a common occurrence. Terrorism plagues nations of peace as the World Trade Center and Pentagon tragedies displayed. Marriages in America fail more often than not, and sickness and disease continue to burden our lives despite technological advances. These maladies among numerous others have left us exhausted, even at our wits' end. We chase one new fad after another in hope of finding answers to our problems. The result is, sad majorities meet the end of their lives full of regret, wishing they had lived differently.

We could spend much time and effort studying the many symptoms of our problems, but this book instead focuses on the root cause of it all. It cuts to the core of our lives, and honestly addresses the reasons why we live with great pain and trouble. We frequently hope the latest study or research report will be the right one to fix our problems, but they never do. If we hope to live victoriously, we *must* come to an understanding of who we are, where we came from, and the source of our trouble. Only then can we overcome the difficulties in our lives, whether they be physical, mental, or spiritual.

Above all, know this: It is absolutely certain you can overcome whatever problem or struggle you're facing. We are meant to be much more than just survivors in life. We are meant to be conquerors over *every* trial, tribulation, and difficulty—NO MATTER WHAT THEY MAY BE! Your success depends on your attitude, and willingness to open your mind to learn the truth about your life and the promises of God.

It is our hope that you will have a determined, humble, and open heart to learn God's will for your life. The pages of this book clearly explain God's promises and instructions on how to overcome *all* trouble, sickness, and pain. It explains God's desire for us to be strong in mind, body, and spirit. Understanding and applying this information to your problems will bring peace, health, and the power to break every stronghold in your life. If you persevere, you *will* absolutely overcome!

Information Source

The reliability of information depends on the validity of its source. Consequently, we have not looked to the latest research report to supply this knowledge because history repeatedly demonstrates a second study will inevitably outdate or refute the first one.

The information you are about to learn comes from one of the oldest and most reliable sources of information known to humankind. More than forty different men from three continents penned this book over a period of approximately 1,500 years. Its prophetic accuracy sets it apart from any other book in history. Its information is infallible, perfect, and no study or report has ever successfully disproved or invalidated its facts. Instead, attempts to discredit this book only work to confirm its uniqueness and accuracy. This book has supernatural power as testified by billions of people over thousands of years. The title of this book literally means *the consecrated book* or *the Holy Book*. Most commonly known, this book is called *The Holy Bible.* The basis for everything you are about to read hasn't originated from any human mind, for *The Holy Bible* reveals the mind of God, not the will of man.

Our thoughts, attitudes, and perceptions often depend on personal experience. We quickly disagree about answers to life's most profound questions as well as the solutions to our most fundamental problems. Consequently, it is much better to ask God about God, than to ask people about God. This is why we rely on the Bible, the word of God, to provide, validate, and explain the information presented in this book.

Please do not misunderstand. We are not asking you to blindly believe information. On the contrary, asking questions is critical, for questions lead to answers, and answers lead to understanding. We are hoping you ask God to teach you what He has revealed in His word because God's knowledge is, in one word, perfect.

All Scripture is given by inspiration of God, and is profitable for doctrine, for reproof, for correction, for instruction in righteousness, that the man of God may be complete, thoroughly equipped for every good work. (2 Timothy 3:16–17)

Make your decision right now to have a persevering spirit that will not rest until it diligently seeks to uncover the truth. Challenge what you know, and do not give up your search until you have received the awesome promises of God. This means the core of your motivation should be to desire what God wants to teach you. It means you must be willing to put your own logic, understanding, knowledge, and experience aside, so that God may have the opportunity to teach you His pure and perfect truth.

Let no one deceive himself. If anyone among you seems to be wise in this age, let him become a fool that he may become wise. (1 Corinthians 3:18)

Making this decision guarantees you will find the knowledge to break free from every sickness, trouble, and difficulty!

"Ask, and it will be given to you; seek, and you will find; knock, and it will be opened to you. For everyone who asks

receives, and he who seeks finds, and to him who knocks it will be opened. Or what man is there among you who, if his son asks for bread, will give him a stone? Or if he asks for a fish, will he give him a serpent? If you then, being evil, know how to give good gifts to your children, how much more will your Father who is in heaven give good things to those who ask Him!" (Matthew 7:7–11)

Yes, if you cry out for discernment, And lift up your voice for understanding, If you seek her as silver, And search for her as for hidden treasures; Then you will understand the fear of the Lord, And find the knowledge of God. For the Lord gives wisdom; From His mouth come knowledge and understanding; (Proverbs 2:3–6)

TESTIMONY: Kate Hannett
Birth Date: December 15, 1974
Occupation: Director of Marketing and Advertising
Experience: **Healed from anxiety, depression, warts, migraines, stomach problems, and fevers**
Date of Testimony: March 2002

Since I was little, my life was plagued with fear and hopelessness. I was afraid of what other people thought about me, afraid to drive, afraid to be alone, and afraid to die. My fears left me paralyzed to do even everyday things like go to the store or even go some place new. As I got older, it grew worse and led me to feelings of depression and hopelessness. I didn't have peace and I was a constant worrier. I figured that life really had no point and nothing really mattered. What was worse is that I grew up thinking I had religion. I thought I knew who God was. But I really never met him. I used to sit in church and wonder, "God, is this really it? If you really are who you say you are, why do I feel this way?"

As I got older, I went to college and met a man who would later become my husband. He was sick with cancer when I met him, and I was very worried about what would happen to him. Then, something changed. After a few months, he didn't worry about his condition or anything else; he finally had peace. I asked him what changed, and he told me that God healed him and took away all his worry.

Of course I did not believe him. Then I thought maybe it was true, but it sounded too strange for me. Why did God heal Steve and why are so many other people still sick? Steve tried to introduce me to the only one who could deliver me from my fears, my anxiety, my depression, and my lack of hope: Jesus Christ.

He explained that Satan is always trying to rob us of our joy and our peace. I didn't want to listen. This scared me. I didn't want to believe that Satan really existed. So I didn't listen to Steve for five whole years! I wouldn't talk about it or think about it. We almost didn't get married because of it.

Then I went through a difficult period in my life. I didn't have a job, I had a lot of things going on, and I still had no peace or hope in my life. So, one weekend (September 1999) I asked Steve to explain the whole story about how God healed him through the power of His precious Son, Jesus Christ. He explained that Satan is at the root of all evil, sickness, worry, and pain. He also explained that I didn't have to be sad or worried because Jesus took all that away when He died on the cross and forgave us for our sins. My burden was lifted! I felt free and happy. But this isn't the end of the story.

After this time, I've had several problems like warts, migraines, fevers, burned fingers, stomach problems, skin rashes, anxiety, and many other things that God totally healed me of! When I asked the doctor what caused the warts he told me it was a virus. When I asked what caused the virus, he said he didn't know. I asked him if I could change my diet so they wouldn't come back, and he said he wasn't sure. The night that I accepted Jesus into my heart, we prayed and cast the evil out that was causing my warts. God was able to take the warts away because His word says so. Even a little thing like warts God does not want us to suffer with. He is the creator of the universe and a loving Father. Why wouldn't he want us to be totally healthy and happy?

He continues to take all my problems away. Any time there is a problem, a bad thought, or an upset feeling or sickness, I ask God to take it away in the name of Jesus Christ because there is power in His Holy name. The only thing I have to do is believe in God's word. I am free. I know God is not a liar. In Isaiah, Chapter 53, it says, "By his stripes we are healed." That's why the cross means so much more to me than just the forgiveness of sins. Jesus suffered, took our pains, and was acquainted with grief so we wouldn't have to be. He loved us so much that He took away the punishment that we deserved. His grace and mercy are abundant. I am so grateful and want to praise His name and give Him all the glory.

Now I live a life full of hope and peace. Not because of anything special I did, but because of what Jesus did on that cross. He has saved me and freed me, and I am free indeed!

Thank you, Lord Jesus Christ, God our Father, and precious Holy Spirit.

Chapter I
The Author of Life

We all have a need to understand where we came from. Sometimes we even go to great lengths to trace our ancestral roots and family trees for more information concerning our identity. Although this knowledge can be valuable, it only scratches the surface of understanding who we are. We must go deeper and travel back in time to the very beginning. Knowing our origin is the best way to understand the world we live in, as well as our current position in life. This is the first step in our journey to learn how to get out from under life's many struggles. So let's begin by answering the age-old question of how we, and the world we live in, came to be.

In the beginning God created the heavens and the earth. (Genesis 1:1)

Yes, believe it or not, this enormous question can be answered in one short sentence. Everything we see, touch, taste, and everything that exists in our world was made by God! Even everything so-called man-made is made of things that God made! In fact...

All things were made through Him, and without Him nothing was made that was made. (John 1:3)

Though many theories attempt to refute this simple truth, consider them carefully. We must remember they are only theories and have never been proven as historical occurrences. Even at the core of every one of these theories still remains the question of where matter came from, and how it came to be organized with such great precision. Every man-made theory unwittingly leads us to the simple truth that if there is a design, there is a designer, and if there is a plan, there is a planner.

> **Then God said, "Let Us make man in Our image, according to Our likeness; let them have dominion over the fish of the sea, over the birds of the air, and over the cattle, over all the earth and over every creeping thing that creeps on the earth." So God created man in His own image; in the image of God He created him; male and female He created them. (Genesis 1:26–27)**

Yes! This is where we have all come from! We were personally created by God in His likeness, not random selection! As babies do not spontaneously come forth from nothing, so we did not spontaneously come forth from nothing. Life came forth from life.

The Way It Was Meant to Be

God made every type of living creature on the earth, but mankind was specially set apart. We were the only part of creation made in the image and likeness of God. We were valued above everything else on earth because we were created as living, spirit-filled beings.

> **And the Lord God formed man of the dust of the ground, and breathed into his nostrils the breath of life; and man became a living being. (Genesis 2:7)**

Adam, unlike every other created being, was given a spirit. This is one of the characteristics that define how we were made in God's image because God Himself is spirit. Then God formed the first woman, Eve, who was a companion and helper for Adam.

> **So Adam gave names to all cattle, to the birds of the air, and to every beast of the field. But for Adam there was not found a helper comparable to him. And the Lord God**

caused a deep sleep to fall on Adam, and he slept; and He took one of his ribs, and closed up the flesh in its place. Then the rib which the Lord God had taken from man He made into a woman, and he brought her to the man. (Genesis 2:20–22)

God loved Adam and Eve, and wanted to give them the best of everything. This is why He placed them in a paradise known as the Garden of Eden.

The Lord God planted a garden eastward in Eden, and there He put the man whom He had formed. (Genesis 2:8)

God not only placed Adam in paradise, but also placed him in a position of great power. A position that gave him authority and dominion over the earth! God privileged Adam to be king of the world!

Then God blessed them, and God said to them, "Be fruitful and multiply; fill the earth and subdue it; have dominion over the fish of the sea, over the birds of the air, and over every living thing that moves on the earth." (Genesis 1:28)

It cannot be stressed enough that the plan and intent of God's heart was to bless (give great things) to Adam and Eve. In the garden, there was no good thing lacking. There was no worry, no weakness, no sickness, and absolutely no disease! Death did not even exist! Adam and Eve were in perfect fellowship with God. The heart of God created a perfect world with perfect unity between Him and His children. This was God's will and intent for mankind. This is the way it was meant to be. So what happened to paradise?

Our Will Created the Way

One of the characteristics of God's creation was, and still is, the freedom to choose and act on our own will. God did not create mindless robots or captive slaves who had no choice but to obey. God never forced His creation to love Him. God created each of us with a will, and gave us the ability to freely act on it. This is one of the reasons why God gave explicit instructions to Adam and Eve not to eat from the tree of the knowledge of good and evil. God gave this command so they would be protected and live in freedom from harm. God wanted to protect them from anything that would prevent them from living in the fullness of His blessing. His exact instructions to Adam were...

> **Then the Lord God took the man and put him in the Garden of Eden to tend and keep it. And the Lord God commanded the man, saying, "Of every tree of the garden you may freely eat; but of the tree of the knowledge of good and evil you shall not eat, for in the day that you eat of it you shall surely die." (Genesis 2:15–17)**

These instructions could not have been clearer. God said to Adam that he had command over everything on earth, but needed to obey God so that no harm would come to him. It was out of God's love for His children that He warned Adam and Eve not to eat the fruit of this tree. This was no trivial matter, for the consequence of disobedience was death!

> **"...for in the day that you eat of it, you shall surely die." (Genesis 2:17)**

God's action is simple to understand since we treat our own children the same way. Even though we'd sometimes like it, we do not have total control over our children. This is why we never hesitate to tell them of the many dangers in the world and continually warn them of the consequences if they disobey. Why? We love them and want to do all that we can to protect them. This scenario is not far from what God did when He warned Adam and Eve not to eat of the tree of the knowledge of good and evil.

The simple act of eating from a tree doesn't seem like that big of a deal. In fact, in today's world, this doesn't seem immoral. Our society says that everything is OK as long as it doesn't hurt someone else. After all they say, "We need to practice tolerance. Truth and morality are relative and are really up to an individual's preference." The difference between our logic and God's understanding, however, is that He knows everything...and we don't. There was obviously much more to the fruit of that tree than was apparent to the natural eye if eating from it would cause their death!

As we will soon see, Adam and Eve forgot that God is almighty (sovereign), all-knowing (omniscient), all-powerful (omnipotent), the beginning and the end, the alpha and the omega, the first and the last.

"I am the Alpha and the Omega, the Beginning and the End, the First and the Last." (Revelation 22:13)

TESTIMONY: Joseph Deragio
Birth Date: April 27, 1960
Occupation: Truck Driver
Experience: **Healed of diabetes**
Date of Testimony: February 3, 1999

Right after my dad was buried, I was out of work for almost three weeks and found out that I had diabetes. The reading was so high it was off the charts. It was past the maximum. I could have gone into a coma and died. I was dizzy, lost my belongings, my driver's license, credit cards, and clothes. I don't know how I drove the truck home that day. I had memory lapses. I was very sick. Everything was going wrong. Master Kim and I read from the Bible, and he taught me God's Word and promises. We prayed together and when I got up, I felt so relieved and relaxed I then drove the truck fine, and was very thankful.

I've also had a physical exam for my new job and no diabetes was found! Not even a trace! My life is finally back on track and I feel great. I feel better and stronger, and I know that God will always be there to help me. For that I am a very grateful person.

Chapter II

Paradise Lost

At the core of free will is always a basic choice. It is the decision of whether we will, or will not, follow the commands of God. There is no middle road offered. We are either moving in a pathway aligned with God or moving in a direction away from God. It is this simple choice that Adam and Eve were faced with in the Garden of Eden.

Despite God's instruction and clear warning, Adam and Eve chose poorly. They put their personal desire before God's command, and ate the fruit of the tree of the knowledge of good and evil. As warned, this caused their spiritual death, and as we will soon see, ultimately brought the world under the control of darkness. Look at the state of our world with all of its hatred and evil, and it will make you think twice about the history of Adam and Eve being just a story of morality. It is the history of humanity, and it's the reason our world exists with great devastation, pain, and agony.

Now you may be thinking, "This isn't fair! It was them who disobeyed, not me! Why do I have to suffer the consequences of *their* actions?" We will carefully consider the reasons, but let's first take a closer look at the consequences of Adam and Eve's tragic decision. Understanding the past will enable us to better understand the solution to our present troubles. It is a critical step in understanding how to break free from all oppression.

As you read, keep in mind that God, our Creator, has provided a way of restoration from the horrible consequences of this great fall. He has provided a way to return to Him, and a way to live free from the consequences of their disobedience!

More Than a Lie

When God gives instruction, He gives it knowing everything in the past, the present, and the future. In fact, there isn't anything that He doesn't know in the entire universe. We, on the other hand, hear God's instruction with extremely limited knowledge of the world we live in. This is why we are often confused concerning the importance of God's commands. Nevertheless, we must realize that if God knows everything, and we don't, it's always in our best interest to trust Him.

In the Garden of Eden, God knew critical information that Adam and Eve didn't know. God knew there was someone else in the garden—someone who represented great danger. His name was Satan. After God commanded Adam and Eve not to eat the fruit of the tree of the knowledge of good and evil, Satan, called the "serpent", visited them.

> Now the serpent was more cunning than any beast of the field which the Lord God had made. And he said to the woman, "Has God indeed said, 'You shall not eat of every tree of the garden'?" And the woman said to the serpent, "We may eat of the fruit of the trees of the garden; but of the fruit of the tree which is in the midst of the garden, God has said, 'You shall not eat it, nor shall you touch it, lest you die.'" Then the serpent said to the woman, "You will not surely die. For God knows that in the day you eat of it your eyes will be opened, and you will be like God, knowing good and evil." So when the woman saw that the tree was good for food, that it was pleasant to the eyes, and a tree desirable to make one wise, she took of its fruit and ate. She also gave to her husband with her, and he ate. (Genesis 3:1–6)

This selection tells a great deal of the events in the garden and reveals what led Eve to eat the fruit. Satan was more cunning than any other living being on earth. This means that he knew *exactly* how to overcome obstacles to get what he wanted. He came to Eve and started what seemed like an innocent conversation asking her what God had commanded. Next, Eve answered Satan's question by accurately quoting God. Then came the fatal deception.

> **Then the serpent said to the woman, "You will not surely die. For God knows that in the day you eat of it your eyes will be opened, and you will be like God, knowing good and evil." (Genesis 3:4–5)**

Satan lied to Eve and told her she was *not* going to die, and then mixed the rest of his response with truth concerning knowing good and evil. Then Eve "*...saw that the tree was good for food, that it was pleasant to the eyes, and a tree desirable to make one wise, she took of its fruit and ate.*"

Eve made two very big mistakes. First she listened to and trusted a voice other than God's. Eve had free will to choose which voice she was going to trust: God's clear instruction saying, "*...you shall surely die.*" (Genesis 2:17), or Satan's voice who said, "*You will not surely die.*" (Genesis 3:4) She chose poorly.

The second big mistake Eve made was she relied on her own resources to make her decision. The Bible says she "*saw*" that it was good. Eve used her judgement and went by the lust of her eye. She put her own knowledge and judgement ahead of God's and followed her desire. Adam made the same mistake by choosing to listen to Eve's voice over God's and chose his desire over God's instruction.

Satan was successful by tempting them to doubt God's word by mixing truth with deception. This led their hearts away from God's desire and toward their own. It was this disobedience that forced God's judgement on their lives. We must be careful to heed the lessons found in Adam and Eve's encounter with Satan so we are not robbed of God's blessing. God is serious when He commands us to

> **Trust in the Lord with all your heart, And lean not on your own understanding; In all your ways acknowledge Him, And He shall direct your paths. (Proverbs 3:5–6)**

The Consequences of Disobedience

When the Bible refers to sin, it means we miss the target of God's will. *Sin*, or *hamartano* translated in Greek, literally means "to miss the mark." It can be compared to missing the goal or bull's eye in archery. Only in this case, the consequences of "missing the mark" were unimaginably devastating. They resulted in Adam and Eve's banishment from paradise, caused their natures to be changed from holy creations to unholy beings, and ultimately placed a curse on every generation to follow. This "fall" from holiness gave opportunity for every form of darkness to enter our world. It accounts for every form of evil, including sickness, disease, and trouble that afflicts our world today!

Separation from Life Meant Death

The first consequence of Adam and Eve's disobedience was separation from God. Never before had they known what it was like to not have complete unity with God. They immediately felt this separation in that they became fearful, anxious, ashamed, and without peace!

> Then the eyes of both of them were opened, and they knew that they were naked; and they sewed fig leaves together and made themselves coverings. And they heard the sound of the Lord God walking in the garden in the cool of the day, and Adam and his wife hid themselves from the presence of the Lord God among the trees of the garden. Then the Lord God called to Adam and said to him, "Where are you?" (Genesis 3:7–9)

Do you see the separation? Adam and Eve were once completely united with God the Father, and the next moment, they were hiding from Him in fear. God even asked, *"Where are you?"* With one question, God brought to light that Adam and Eve were the ones who moved, and they were no longer walking with Him. For the first time in their lives they were alone and were no longer "joined" with

... ource of all life! It was this separation from God's life-giving spirit that caused their spiritual death. Tragically, this "breaking away" from life meant a joining to darkness that has continued through every generation to present. This means that every person is born into this world spiritually separated from God. Yes, that even means you and me!

> **Therefore, just as through one man sin entered the world, and death through sin, and thus death spread to all men, because all sinned. (Romans 5:12)**

We can see that death reigned according to the likeness of Adam's sin.

> **Nevertheless death reigned from Adam to Moses, even over those who had not sinned according to the likeness of the transgression of Adam, who is a type of Him who was to come. (Romans 5:14)**

Like many, you may be wondering how we can start our lives in darkness before we ever have a chance to make a mistake. After all, how can we say that we are spiritually dead if we are created in the likeness of God? The answer is clearly explained. Read the following verses slowly and see the critical distinction between the creation of Adam and the creation of everyone after.

First, we see that God made Adam in His likeness.

> **This is the book of the genealogy of Adam. In the day that God created man, He made him in the likeness of God. He created them male and female, and blessed them and called them Mankind in the day they were created. (Genesis 5:1–2)**

Then, after Adam was born, and became spiritually separated from God, everyone was made in *Adam*'s image!

> **And Adam lived one hundred and thirty years, and begot a son in his own likeness, after his image, and named him Seth. (Genesis 5:3)**

If someone asked for the name of a person's grandfather, most would have little trouble answering. If asked the name of their great-, great-,

great-, great-, great-, great-grandfather, most wouldn't have a clue. Amazingly, we now know the name of our very first grandfather was Adam. The Bible makes it clear that we come from him and have inherited his fallen, corrupt, and sinful nature along with every one of his weaknesses!

We sometimes have trouble accepting this truth because we figure that we were not responsible for the fall. We say, "It wasn't our fault that Adam and Eve fell. Maybe Adam and Eve were separated from God, but I'm a good person, and I believe that God is just and fair, and I am already spiritually connected to Him." Well, it is true that we were not physically in the Garden of Eden, but the fact is that Adam is the father of mankind. We cannot escape the decisions he and Eve made, and the consequences that affected every generation after them.

To illustrate this point, let's consider DNA, the genetic blueprint for our bodies. We know that a mother and a father carry a unique set of characteristics contained in their DNA, and when they have a baby, their characteristics are passed down to their children. The child possesses the very same characteristics as his or her parents. In the same way, sin and this spiritual separation from God have been passed down from one generation to the next. The fruit of a tree is only as pure and healthy as the branch from which it grows. Think of it, how could a spiritually living person be born from two spiritually dead people? Obviously, two spiritually dead people give birth to a spiritually dead child.

Let's consider another example. When a mother carries a child in her womb, the baby shares the mother's experiences. Whatever the mother eats, the child eats. Whatever the mother takes in her body, the baby takes in his or her body. The mother's actions determine the future health of her child. In the same way, Adam and Eve's actions determined our future.

We even see evidence of Adam and Eve's fallen characteristics in the actions of people both young and old. Though little children appear completely pure and innocent to the natural eye, simple observation reveals a different story. Parents have to teach babies not to be selfish, not to hit their brothers and sisters, and not to be greedy and self-centered. Even psychologists have studied that children at a very young age cannot understand any need separate from their own. These characteristics reflect the actions of sinful nature rather than the selfless love of God's holy nature. Even older children need school rules, education on how to live with one another, and adults need laws to prevent us from stealing and killing each other! Please understand this is not to say that we do not have the potential for good, it just demonstrates that our "natural natures" do not reflect the ways of God. They are tainted and poisoned with sin.

It may be easy to blame Adam and Eve and shake our fists at them, but when we honestly look at ourselves, have we not done the same thing as them? Have we not known the difference between right and wrong in many situations, and willfully chosen wrong? In addition, not one person since the Garden of Eden has ever perfectly obeyed *all* of God's law except Jesus Christ, the Son of God. We have *all* fallen short of God's law in some way. We have all missed the mark sometime or another. Expressed another way, we are *all* sinners in the eyes of God.

> **...for all have sinned and fall short of the glory of God,...**
> **(Romans 3:23)**

Notice the tense used in this verse. We "have sinned" referring to the past, and "fall" referring to the present. We are all guilty of sin!

Though unpleasant to face this reality, we must confront it if we hope to partake in God's solution. We must not shy back and accept falsehood for the sake of comfort. Many have chosen to follow "feel-good" philosophies, but often still confess they lack peace. No matter what they do, they cannot fill the empty void in their lives. They try everything the world can offer, including religion, money, fame, sex, education, and drugs, but never find true peace and happiness. The "sin" problem still remains because none of these things can fix our separation from God. The attitude of choosing our own way will not and cannot change what God has clearly communicated to us.

But your iniquities have separated you from your God; And your sins have hidden His face from you, So that He will not hear. (Isaiah 59:2)

Things are not what we want them to be, they are what they are. As we will soon learn, only by following God's clear instruction can we find the peace we so desperately need and yearn for.

The Blind Cannot Lead Themselves

Another consequence of the great fall is spiritual blindness. This means that we are automatically able to perceive and understand our physical world, but are born blind to the things in the spiritual world. We understand the laws of nature, but are "blind" and "ignorant" to the things of God.

But the natural man does not receive the things of the Spirit of God, for they are foolishness to him; nor can he know them, because they are spiritually discerned. (1 Corinthians 2:14)

There was no philosophy or debate about truth in the Garden of Eden. Truth was self-evident and easy to understand. Adam and Eve had no difficulty understanding God, and it wasn't until Satan tempted Adam and Eve to doubt the validity of God's instruction that they began to question what they already knew. When they died spiritually, they no longer had the ability to "see" truth, and were easily led astray.

Think about the answers to these simple questions. If we were able to clearly see spiritual truths, and weren't spiritually blind, why would we need to search for it? Why would there be debate? Why would men create so many religions that teach completely contradictory views? The answer is that we are born lacking spiritual sight and understanding. We come into the world completely oblivious to the truth that created us. Many adopt the religion of their parents never really knowing if it's *the* truth from God. To make matters even worse, Satan is still working to deceive the whole world!

> So the great dragon was cast out, that serpent of old, called
> the Devil and Satan, who deceives the whole world... (Rev-
> elation 12:9)

The first step Satan takes to deceive is to keep us from ever
hearing *the* truth found in the Bible. If unsuccessful, he then attempts
to get us to doubt the truth found in the Bible. This was exactly how
he deceived Adam and Eve. He lured their focus away from God's
word and toward his lies, ultimately leading them to destruction.
Satan is relentless in his pursuit to make us doubt the validity of
God's word. He knows that if we begin to understand and live according to every word that proceeds from the mouth of God (Matthew 4:4), he will lose control over us. No wonder the Bible is one of
the most widely printed and purchased books in the world, but one
of the least read! The fact is that if we do not read the word of God,
we do not understand God's truth, and it is therefore impossible to
follow it! This is why Satan so easily keeps many bound to low living. When you make your decision to heed God's instructions for
your life, you will infallibly protect yourself from being tricked,
duped, and deceived by Satan!

A New King in the World

Another devastating consequence of the great fall is that Adam
lost his position in the world. We already saw during creation that
God literally gave him the world. He gave Adam and Eve authority
in the earth and over all things in the earth! Unbeknownst to many,
our original position in the world was that of a "king," a ruler with
power and authority given by God.

> Then God blessed them, and God said to them, "Be fruit-
> ful and multiply; fill the earth and subdue it; have domin-
> ion over the fish of the sea, over the birds of the air, and
> over every living thing that moves on the earth." (Genesis
> 1:28)

Adam and Eve were given this privilege by God and were not self-
proclaimed rulers. They always answered to the sovereignty of God

and were given clear instruction to follow. When they used their authority improperly, they not only lost their spiritual life but also fell from their God-given position.

"...Truly, this only I have found: That God made man upright, But they have sought out many schemes." (Ecclesiastes 7:29)

When Adam and Eve made the decision to follow the serpent instead of God, they in essence chose to be led by another authority. It is this authority that mankind became enslaved to. Adam, Eve, and all generations to follow were literally brought *under* the power of the prince of darkness called Satan. This makes perfect sense. No longer joined to the light of life, Adam and Eve were no longer legitimate children of the living God, and became enslaved children of darkness. Truly, God warned Adam and Eve that they would die!

The right to be "King of the World" was a privilege given to mankind, and it was taken away as a consequence of their disobedience. Many wonder why God created a world filled with sickness, disease, pain, rape, suffering, murder, and torment. The answer is simple: God didn't! God created a beautiful and perfect world with no pain at all. We were the ones who opened the door to destruction! Adam and Eve willfully allowed Satan the opportunity to usurp the position of "King of the Earth."

The fact that Satan is "King of the World" is demonstrated in the Bible when Satan offered Jesus the kingdoms of the world.

Then the devil, taking Him up on a high mountain, showed Him all the kingdoms of the world in a moment of time. And the devil said to Him, "All this authority I will give You, and their glory; for this has been delivered to me, and I give it to whomever I wish..." (Luke 4:5–6)

How could Satan offer to Jesus what he did not already possess? Yes, power and authority on earth were delivered to Satan when he successfully tempted Adam and Eve to fall. Even one of his names is the "prince of the power of the air," revealing his jurisdiction in this world. Note that it is his spirit who is working in the sons of disobedience (those who have not been reunited with God).

> ...according to the prince of the power of the air, the spirit
> who now works in the sons of disobedience... (Ephesians
> 2:2)

The Bible is very clear that Satan not only has possession of this
world, but also of *those* who are *still* separated from God. We can see
that people (exactly like Adam and Eve) "belong" to the devil during the time they are in sin.

> He who sins is of the devil, for the devil has sinned from
> the beginning... (1 John 3:8)

Even Jesus Christ, the Son of God, explicitly addressed men whose
hearts were far from God as having a different father. Their father
was the devil.

> Jesus said to them, "If God were your Father, you would
> love Me, for I proceeded forth and came from God; nor
> have I come of Myself, but He sent Me. Why do you not
> understand My speech? Because you are not able to listen
> to My word. You are of your father the devil, and the de-
> sires of your father you want to do. He was a murderer
> from the beginning, and does not stand in the truth, be-
> cause there is no truth in him. When he speaks a lie, he
> speaks from his own resources, for he is a liar and the fa-
> ther of it." (John 8:42–44)

> "I will deliver you from the *Jewish* people, as well as *from*
> the Gentiles, to whom I now send you, to open their eyes,
> *in order* to turn *them* from darkness to light, and *from* the
> power of Satan to God, that they may receive forgiveness
> of sins and an inheritance among those who are sanctified
> by faith in Me." (Acts 26:17–18)

Truly there are only two kinds of people in the world. Those who
are slaves of evil, and those who have been reunited with God, called
the children of God. Those currently held captive by sin must come
to God so that they can be freed from the chains of darkness.

> And a servant of the Lord must not quarrel but be gentle
> to all, able to teach, patient, in humility correcting those
> who are in opposition, if God perhaps will grant them

repentance, so that they may know the truth, and that they may come to their senses and escape the snare of the devil, having been taken captive by him to do his will. (2 Timothy 2:24–26)

Do you not know that to whom you present yourselves slaves to obey, you are that one's slaves whom you obey, whether of sin leading to death, or of obedience leading to righteousness? (Romans 6:16)

Do not think for one second that Satan was lifted high in any way by usurping this position. On the contrary, Satan is more cursed than anything else the Lord has made, and received ultimate condemnation.

So the Lord God said to the serpent, "Because you have done this, You are cursed more than all cattle, And more than every beast of the field; On your belly you shall go, And you shall eat dust All the days of your life. And I will put enmity Between you and the woman, And between your seed and her Seed; He shall bruise your head, And you shall bruise His heel." (Genesis 3:14–15).

Here we see Satan is destined for never-ending, eternal punishment.

The devil, who deceived them, was cast into the lake of fire and brimstone where the beast and the false prophet are. And they will be tormented day and night forever and ever. (Revelation 20:10)

Now that we understand that Satan is King of our present world, look again at the surrounding trouble, and it becomes easy to understand why things are so bad. Everything evil, bad, painful, hurtful, and destructive is a testament that Satan is here among us.

"The thief does not come except to steal, and to kill, and to destroy..." (John 10:10)

Thank God that ever since judgement fell on Adam and Eve, God set a plan in motion to restore His children to Himself. We will soon understand the "Way" back to God, but let's first take a closer look at our enemy.

TESTIMONY: Joyce Torara
Occupation: Financial Sales
Experience: **Healed of Epstein-Barr (Chronic Fatigue Syndrome)**
Date of Testimony: September 1999

All my life I've had more energy than any of my friends and family members. I've always pushed myself and to top it off I never really slept. By this I mean I could survive with three to four hours of sleep a night and still function with the same level of enthusiasm as the day before. If I ran out of things to do, I would clean and reclean. In August of 1999, all activity ceased. I no longer went to the gym or did anything remotely close to exercise. I was simply exhausted and would come home from work and just sit around. I didn't even have the strength to clean. My husband noticed I did not resemble myself and knows me well enough to know that I am not lazy. I reluctantly went to see my doctor in October. He proceeded to tell me that I had Epstein-Barr virus and it's forever. There is no cure. I will just have to deal with it. Stress can trigger it and my immune system when low. In other words, I was susceptible to anything that came my way such as colds, other viruses, etc. Although I no longer attended Tae Kwon Do classes, due to moving out of NJ, I kept in touch with one of the Black Belt instructors, Steve Hannett. One day out the blue, Steve called me just to say hi. I explained to him what was going on in my life. I told him that it's not going to get me down & I will beat it on my own. Steve then said to me that I don't have to do it on my own and that I could ask God's help. And His help would be the cure. I met with Steve in person one Sunday. We spent the day reacquainting me with my faith in Jesus Christ. To truly believe in Jesus Christ would allow myself to beat the demons, which were the major players in situations that allow us to get sick or hurt. Steve then prayed for me. Now, I'm the ideal skeptic and if I didn't feel the energy myself, I would never believe it. As Steve was praying over me, I felt a cramp in my chest. I thought at first that I was just getting tired of standing but Steve explained that it was the demons leaving my body. After that day I was back to my old self. I'm back to the gym, I outrun my nieces and nephews, and I'm a cleaning fool again. I know now that Steve called me for a reason. God knew that I needed some guidance.

Chapter III
The Evil One Unmasked

Understanding the devil's influence in our world is critical to overcoming our trials and tribulations. Many people, and even churches, do not want to talk about Satan due to fear, false expectation, and the desire to be politically correct. God, however, is very clear that we must live by every word that proceeds from His mouth. This means that we must be willing to study and follow the entirety of God's Word, including the study of Satan.

Satan is probably one of the least understood characters in the Bible and the world. People often think of a red figure with horns and a tail, but this is definitely not an accurate view of his identity. Hollywood either trivializes the devil to appear cute and harmless or portrays him to be much more powerful than he is. These extremes are seen in daily life when parents allow their children to dress up as the devil for Halloween, while others are so afraid of him they won't dare say his name. Truly, we have a faulty understanding of the origin, character, and daily working of Satan. Consequently, let's explore Satan's origin, his works, and his motivation in the world.

The Beginning of Darkness

Many believe that the creation of the world marked the beginning of time, but this isn't so. God already had an established kingdom before the foundation of the world (earth).

> Lord, You have been our dwelling place in all generations.
> Before the mountains were brought forth, Or ever You had
> formed the earth and the world, Even from everlasting to
> everlasting, You are God. (Psalm 90:1–2)

God's kingdom contained angels, who served God day and night. These angels were given the gift of free will just as Adam and Eve. One angel, named Lucifer, was given a position of power and authority in God's kingdom. His name meant "son of dawn," or the "morning light," and he was holy and glorious in God's kingdom. Unfortunately, Lucifer made a freewill decision to put himself at enmity with God. He no longer desired to be a servant of God, but only wanted to be served by others. Lucifer became prideful and wanted to overthrow God's throne so that he himself could become king. In short, he wanted to be like God! The prophet Isaiah gives us insight to Lucifer's desires.

> "For you have said in your heart: 'I will ascend into heaven,
> I will exalt my throne above the stars of God; I will also sit
> on the mount of the congregation On the farthest sides of
> the north; I will ascend above the heights of the clouds, I
> will be like the Most High.'" (Isaiah 14:13–14)

Lucifer desired in his heart, at the very core of his being, to exalt himself to a place where he had no privilege. As amazing as it sounds, one-third of God's angels followed Lucifer in this rebellion, and a great war resulted in heaven. Lucifer and one-third of the angels who followed him were utterly defeated and thrown out of heaven never to return!

> And war broke out in heaven: Michael and his angels
> fought with the dragon; and the dragon and his angels
> fought, but they did not prevail, nor was a place found for
> them in heaven any longer. (Revelation 12:7–8)

> And another sign appeared in heaven: behold, a great, fi-
> ery red dragon having seven heads and ten horns, and
> seven diadems on his heads. His tail drew a third of the
> stars of heaven and threw them to the earth. And the
> dragon stood before the woman who was ready to give

birth, to devour her Child as soon as it was born. (Revelation 12:3–4)

We see that Lucifer's actions, along with one-third of the stars (angels), caused them to be judged, sentenced, and condemned.

> "How you are fallen from heaven, O Lucifer, son of the morning! How you are cut down to the ground, You who weakened the nations! For you have said in your heart: 'I will ascend into heaven, I will exalt my throne above the stars of God; I will also sit on the mount of the congregation. On the farthest sides of the north; I will ascend above the heights of the clouds, I will be like the Most High.' Yet you shall be brought down to Sheol, to the lowest depths of the Pit. Those who see you will gaze at you, and consider you, saying: 'Is this the man who made the earth tremble, Who shook kingdoms, who made the world as a wilderness and destroyed its cities, who did not open the house of his prisoners?'" (Isaiah 14:12–17)

When Lucifer sinned against God, his destiny was forever altered. His name was changed to Satan, literally meaning "the adversary," and he was estranged from God for all eternity. Satan's nature changed so that he no longer reflected the glory of God, but became devoid of God's light, leaving only darkness. This change also held true for one-third of the angels who followed Satan. Their natures were changed from servants of light to servants of darkness. This is why they are referred to as fallen angels. They are purely evil with absolutely no good in them. They are darkness and in them there is no light. This is contrasted to the nature of God where the Bible says,

> This is the message which we have heard from Him and declare to you, that God is light and in Him is no darkness at all. (1 John 1:5)

Watch Out! He's in the World

Knowing where Satan came from may seem academic until we realize where he resides today. When Satan and one-third of the angels were judged, and God cast them out of heaven, where were they sent?

> **So the great dragon was cast out, that serpent of old, called the Devil and Satan, who deceives the whole world; he was cast to the earth, and his angels were cast out with him. (Revelation 12:9)**

Yes! They were actually sent to earth and are still here among us! The devil and the fallen angels are on the earth causing all the pain, destruction, and deception in the entire world.

> **"Therefore rejoice, O heavens, and you who dwell in them! Woe to the inhabitants of the earth and the sea! For the devil has come down to you, having great wrath, because he knows that he has a short time." (Revelation 12:12)**

The Bible explicitly warns that the devil has come down to us, and has great wrath. Here is another instance where we learn that Satan is on earth.

> **And the Lord said to Satan, "From where do you come?" So Satan answered the Lord and said, "From going to and fro on the earth, and from walking back and forth on it." (Job 1:7)**

Satan is not in another dimension or mystical place. He is not an abstract concept of that which is "not good." He is an actual being that is here walking among us with only one goal in mind: to destroy. No wonder the Bible says:

> **See then that you walk circumspectly, not as fools but as wise, redeeming the time, because the days are evil. (Ephesians 5:15)**

Satan Exposed

One of the biggest misperceptions of Satan is that he is somehow equal to God in knowledge and power. This world (under Satan's sway) portrays God and Satan as each other's nemesis with equal strength, stature, and position. Nothing could be further from the truth! The struggle between good and evil is never synonymous with a struggle between God and Satan. God does not struggle with Satan. God is so far greater than Satan that He only need command evil and evil obeys. There is never an instance where God Himself wrestles with Satan. God is far more powerful than Satan for this to ever happen. As you will soon see, the struggle between good and evil is waged on a different level.

Satan is neither omniscient nor omnipotent. He is by no means all-knowing or all-powerful like God. He does not have any power in and of himself and cannot be in more than one place at a time. Satan is the father of lies, a murderer, the destroyer of hope, a thief, the accuser, and most of all, an adversary of mankind! Despite his limitations, we must recognize that he is a master of understanding how to overcome obstacles to get what he wants, especially if that means separating you from God! Remember...

Now the serpent was more cunning than any beast of the field which the Lord God had made... (Genesis 3:1)

Satan is filled with a wrath toward God that we cannot comprehend. He knows there is nothing in his future but eternal torment. In the following verse, we can see a description of Satan's nature, and the fact that he is the exact antithesis of the heavenly Father.

"...He was a murderer from the beginning, and does not stand in the truth, because there is no truth in him. When he speaks a lie, he speaks from his own resources, for he is a liar and the father of it." (John 8:44)

Understanding God is the giver of life, and Satan is the destroyer of life, completely changes our perspective on our problems! It shatters the façade and deception we have lived under for so long. Whenever you see the birth, growth, and blessing of life, God is there. When you see murder, death, and sickness, Satan is there. Accordingly, wherever there is truth, God is there, and wherever there is a lie, Satan is there. Remember...

...God is light and in Him is no darkness at all. (1 John 1:5)

"The thief does not come except to steal, and to kill, and to destroy. I have come that they may have life, and that they may have it more abundantly." (John 10:10)

Everything Satan says is a lie, and diametrically opposed to the love of God. His nature is to deceive and continuously disguise his lies to appear like truth. He understands how to prevent us from focusing on God, and does all that he can to keep us separated from Him. When we follow Satan's doctrine, we give him permission to run havoc in our lives. Every philosophy, attitude, doctrine, and teaching that does not come from God the Father is essentially satanic. Yes, everything that is against God and against His truth in the Bible is satanic. Giving heed to the concept that all religion is the same, and it doesn't matter what you follow, is choosing to listen to the very voice of Satan. How could the supposed "God" of different philosophies and religions be the same? Their doctrines and very descriptions of God are so different from one another it makes this impossible! It is only that we know so little about the truth and these false religions that we have been led astray. Through the ages, men and women under the influence of Satan have developed their own belief systems, creating false ideas and perceptions about God. Every attempt to create new truth is futile. We must be careful not to be tricked into playing the role of a creator. God alone is creator, not us.

Truth contains absolutely no error or falsehood. This means that there can only be one truth. If two things claim to be true, and they are the opposite of one another, how can they both be right? The answer is, they can't. The devil has tricked us into believing that the differences between religions and philosophies don't matter. We shrug our shoulders and casually say, "It's all the same anyway." The spine-chilling reality is that except for the Bible, no other religion or philosophy tells you the truth about Satan. In fact, many, if not most, religions don't even mention the existence of Satan! Those very few that do, conceal his true identity and never reveal how to defeat him! Satan is hiding! This is why he deceives with false religions and doesn't want people to learn *that* the truth has power to set us free and overcome him!

> **So the great dragon was cast out, that serpent of old, called the Devil and Satan, who deceives the whole world; he was cast to the earth, and his angels were cast out with him. (Revelation 12:9)**

When we refuse to learn and trust God's word, we allow Satan to deceive us. Knowing this, and realizing that Satan's *only* desire is to kill, steal, and destroy, should be more than enough motivation to run to God.

The main point to grasp, and never let go of, is that ignoring the reality of Satan is to ignore the very root of all suffering, pain, sickness, and tragedy! The great news, however, is that God is so far exalted above Satan, our minds cannot fully comprehend it. Satan is always under the control and authority of our sovereign God. There is never a power struggle between God and Satan. There is never a contest. Lucifer only said in his heart that he wanted to take God's position and was kicked out of heaven. God is creator, and Satan only a creation, existing underneath the sovereign power of Almighty God. This should give us great confidence that God, who is for us, is much greater than the devil who is against us.

> **What then shall we say to these things? If God is for us, who can be against us? (Romans 8:31)**

> **You are of God, little children, and have overcome them, because He who is in you is greater than he who is in the world. (1 John 4:4)**

The key is to understand how to make sure we are "connected" to God, and how to use His power to overcome the devil! The Bible provides greater detail concerning Satan's nature and character, but this basic information is sufficient to understand the root of trouble in our world.

Now for the tough question: If God is a loving God with supreme power, how could He allow evil to rule the earth and cause such great pain? Read on for God's answer.

TESTIMONY: Peter DeJesus
Birth Date: June 1, 1963
Occupation: Financial Planner
Experience: **Healed of a wrist injury and ankle injury**
Date of Testimony: February 2001

The nature of my problem began back in July 2000. While at the gym working out, I sprained my wrist doing wrist curls. The pain was so bad I couldn't bend it or even hold a grocery bag. For two months, I used a wrist support & sports cream to help the pain. During this time, I regained some mobility but the pain was still there. I was still having difficulties doing simple exercises like pushups and rotating my wrists.

Master Kim kept asking if I was all right. I told him not to worry. I'll be fine. Around October of 2000, Master Kim introduced me to the Bible. We discussed many topics such as my faith, the love of Jesus Christ, and why He died for us. We also talked about the power of prayer and faith in Jesus Christ. After this session was over, I discovered my faith was not as strong as I thought it was.

It was about this same time that the pain in my wrist became worse. I could not withhold the pain any longer. I finally gave in and asked Master Kim for guidance. Master Kim discussed the love that Jesus has for us, and the demons that surround us all. We prayed hard together. Master Kim told me to confess my sins to Jesus and ask for his forgiveness. At the same time, Master Kim was commanding the demon to leave my body and to never return. This experience was very emotional but by the end of the prayer my pain was gone.

While sparring back in December 2000, I sprained my ankle. This time I couldn't even walk without an ankle support. I barely made it through my belt test and passed. I tried different sports creams, and even took painkillers to stop the pain. As the weeks went on, Master Kim would ask if everything was good. Of course I told him not to worry. The truth was I didn't want to trouble Master Kim with my problems. By mid-January of 2001, I couldn't stand the pain anymore. The pain was affecting my training and personal life. Since the injury, my wife told me to tell Master Kim about my problem. I finally gave in and asked

Master Kim for his guidance once again. He asked if I had been praying since the last session; I said no. He also asked me if I was keeping up with my Bible readings; I said no. Because my faith was so weak, I was an easy target for the demons to attack my body again.

Through strong prayer and guidance from Master Kim, Jesus Christ healed me once again. But before I left, Master Kim told me to pray every day, go to church on Sundays, and read the scriptures as often as possible. If my faith was strong, these occurrences would not have lasted as long as they did. As weeks go by, my faith will become stronger. I now attend church more frequently with my family. I have also started to reinforce my faith with Bible lessons provided by Master Kim. I cannot and will not lose faith on the one who died for me—Jesus Christ. Thank you, Jesus Christ, for healing my pain, my heart, and guiding me to the right path.

Chapter IV

Evil's Jurisdiction

Now for the age-old question: How could our loving God allow Satan to torment this world? To understand the answer, we must closely examine God's judgements of Satan, Adam, and Eve in the Garden of Eden.

To review, we know that Satan desired and previously attempted to become king of God's kingdom and failed. In addition, we know that he was banished to earth (Revelation 12:9), and that he is filled with great wrath against God and His creation (Revelation 12:12). Given this information, it is clear why Satan devised a scheme to cause Adam and Eve to disobey God's command. Satan desired to become king of the world, and knew he needed to overthrow Adam, the current king.

At the time of Satan's attempted takeover, he did not have the power to destroy Adam because power and authority on earth was already given to Adam. Thus, it was necessary for Satan to devise a plan. From experience, Satan understood that the way to remove God's power and authority from Adam was to get him to disobey God's command. He knew Adam and Eve's disobedience would cause their holy natures to change and become dark like his own.

The Curse Examined

God is righteous. Every word that proceeds from His mouth is perfect and pure. Accordingly, God must follow through and take action on everything He says. To deny His own word would be to deny Himself. This is why God had to follow through with His judgement of the events in the Garden of Eden on all guilty parties: Satan, Adam, and Eve. God judged Satan and said,

> **So the Lord God said to the serpent: "Because you have done this, You are cursed more than all cattle, And more than every beast of the field; On your belly you shall go, And you shall eat dust all the days of your life. And I will put enmity Between you and the woman, And between your seed and her Seed; He shall bruise your head, And you shall bruise His heel." (Genesis 3:14–15)**

This is the second time God judged Satan. The first occurred when Satan desired to exalt himself above God and was thrown out of heaven. Now because of his deceptive actions, God mandated that Satan would be destroyed. God prophetically revealed that there would be One who would ultimately destroy Him.

> **"...He shall bruise your head, And you shall bruise His heel." (Genesis 3:15)**

Before his final judgement would be carried out, he was cursed to do something, which at first glance appears rather strange. Satan was cursed to *"eat dust all the days of his life."*

> **"...On your belly you shall go, and you shall eat dust all the days of your life." (Genesis 3:14)**

What is the "dust?" Is Satan, a spiritual being, cursed to eat dry dirt? No! The answer to what the "dust" is can be found within God's judgement of Adam.

> **Then to Adam He said, "Because you have heeded the voice of your wife, and have eaten from the tree of which I commanded you, saying, 'You shall not eat of it': Cursed is the ground for your sake; In toil you shall eat of it All the days of your life. Both thorns and thistles It shall bring forth for you, And you shall eat the herb of the field. In the sweat of your face you shall eat bread Till you return to the ground, for out of it you were taken; For dust you are, And to dust you shall return." (Genesis 3:17–19)**

Look very closely and you will see the answer. God told Satan, *"You shall eat dust all the days of your life."* (Genesis 3:14) Then He told Adam, *"For dust you are."* (Genesis 3:19) God told Satan to eat *dust,* and then told Adam that he was the *dust*! Believe it or not...we are the dust! As a consequence of the great fall from holiness, a curse was placed on humanity. The devil now has the right "to eat" our flesh! This is why Satan is allowed to try to harm and destroy each of us. This is why the Bible says,

> **Be sober, be vigilant; because your adversary the devil walks about like a roaring lion, seeking whom he may devour. (1 Peter 5:8)**

You and I have to face the reality that we have a spiritual enemy looking to destroy us. This is why our lives are plagued with trouble. Satan "eats" or "devours" us using any and all means feasible, including sickness, disease, accidents, mental problems, and anything and everything that harms and causes destruction! This means the root of sickness and your particular problem is caused by the devil. No matter what malady you may be suffering from, the root of the problem is spiritual, and not physical! Remember...

> **"The thief does not come except to steal, and to kill, and to destroy..." (John 10:10)**

This makes perfect sense! Before the devil had any power on earth, there was no sickness or disease. After the devil usurped Adam's power, there was murder, sickness, pain, and great trouble on earth. When we look at heaven, where the devil cannot reside, there is no sickness, pain, or suffering of any kind. This means where the devil is, there is pain. Where the devil is not, there is peace and joy. Now we can better understand what we read earlier,

> **"...Woe to the inhabitants of the earth and the sea! For the devil has come down to you, having great wrath, because he knows that he has a short time." (Revelation 12:12)**

It's easy to look with physical or "natural" eyes at this world and see bacteria, carcinogens, and viruses. It may seem like they're the root cause of sickness, but they are only symptoms. They are only the physical manifestations of the problem. Doctors and medical practitioners do an efficient job of measuring and examining the symptoms of disease, but these methods do not and cannot detect the spiritual cause behind them. The Bible accurately unveils the invisible catalyst behind visible symptoms. No wonder Satan doesn't want us to read it!

A critical key in overcoming your sickness or problem is that you must look with spiritual eyes, past the physical, and into the spiritual root. Though men and women have made incredible technological breakthroughs, and science is advancing faster than ever, there is still no cure for sickness...not even the common cold! Medication and treatments only serve to relieve or hold back the symptoms of a disease. Even when symptoms subside, can drug medications address the deeper spiritual problem? In more cases than not, people are forced to trade one set of problems from a disease for a whole other set of problems from the treatment! We call them side effects. It is a well-known fact that these side effects often cause great pain, discomfort, and sometimes irreparable damage.

Take for example cancer, which is commonly treated with radiation and/or chemotherapy (chemical drug therapy). Although these treatments help retard the growth of tumors, they never actually cure cancer. In fact, most doctors wish to examine cancer patients for five to seven years following treatment to check if the disease has begun to rear its ugly head again. The truth is that it was never really gone to begin with because the spiritual root of the problem was never addressed. To make matters worse, many medications and drug treatments are literally poison to the human body! Even women who are pregnant are highly discouraged from taking any medication for fear of harm to the baby. If it harms the baby, what is it doing to us? Drugs and other treatments can never successfully stop the devil from causing harm. We cannot win this spiritual battle with fleshly, physical means. The strongholds in our lives must be pulled down with weapons far greater in strength.

For though we walk in the flesh, we do not war according to the flesh. For the weapons of our warfare are not carnal but mighty in God for pulling down strongholds. (2 Corinthians 10:3–4)

The point is that apart from God, we really do not understand how to deal with our problems. Please do not misunderstand. Doctors have good intentions and, in some instances, are very useful. However, the fact remains that the world's methods for healing will always remain limited. Trying to fix the pain in our world while neglecting the knowledge and power of God is futile! They will never bring the freedom we yearn for.

The July 26, 2000 issue of the *Journal of the American Medical Association* (volume 284) states that the activity of modern medicine accounts for the third leading cause of death in the United States following behind heart disease and cancer. The article states that 250,000 deaths per year are due to iatrogenic causes. Iatrogenic causes are defined as induced in a patient by a physician's activity, manner, or therapy. Some examples of these are unnecessary surgery, medication, errors in hospitals, infections in hospitals, and negative effects of drugs.

Many medical professionals themselves testify that they are unable to treat sickness and disease as effectively as they hope to. They clearly admit that their answers could never match the effectiveness of God's solution. So many suffer and die simply due to a lack of knowledge of how to stand strong against the workings of Satan. God even says:

"My people are destroyed for lack of knowledge." (Hosea 4:6)

Reason dictates that we should judge the truthfulness of something because of its results, and not personal opinion. People who have trusted God's way to overcome Satan in their lives have been delivered from him and are healed!

I, Steve Hannett, personally testify to this fact because I was a cancer patient, received radiation, and felt its horrible side effects.

Then I learned the very information you are reading right now and acted on God's solution to overcome the evil which caused my cancer. As a result, I was healed of cancer and recovered 100 percent! This very same testimony has happened to literally thousands upon thousands! I have seen dozens upon dozens myself, and we have provided only a small sampling of these stories in this book. (Please see chapter 13.)

The key is to understand God's "Way" of restoration to freedom. If not, every person, no matter who they may be, is stuck in the condition and consequences of their sin. You must understand how to break free!

> **Trust in the Lord with all your heart, And lean not on your own understanding; In all your ways acknowledge Him, And He shall direct your paths. Do not be wise in your own eyes; Fear the Lord and depart from evil. It will be health to your flesh, And strength to your bones. (Proverbs 3:5–8)**

TESTIMONY: Eleanor Vick
Birth Date: February 7, 1954
Occupation: Grade School Teacher
Experience: **Healed of degenerative arthritis and osteoarthritis**
Date of Testimony: June 30, 1997

For the past 6 years I have suffered with degenerative arthritis in both hands, and for the past year I've experienced the early stages of osteoarthritis in both hips. It has caused pain and swelling in these joints and my hands were becoming disfigured. Doctors told me that the symptoms could be managed with anti-inflammatory medication, but they could only treat the symptoms, not cure the disease. The medication made me ill, and I took it only when the pain was acute.

When I met Master Kim, I could tell he was a very spiritual man, but I in no way expected to realize the true nature of his spirituality. Upon hearing of my illness Master Kim assured me that the disease was not mine. This confused me since I was the one with the pain and discomfort. He asked to meet with me and my husband, saying he could help. I was willing to try anything that could bring relief. Master Kim talked to us about our religious beliefs and spoke about the creator and the devil. He explained his study of various religions but only believes in the Bible and Jesus Christ as being the truth. During the session I was experiencing pain in my hands and hips. We read selections from the Bible about the casting out of demons by Jesus in order to cure various people of their illnesses. This is when Master Kim's earlier statement made sense. That demons within us cause our suffering and that we can be cured by driving them out.

We read several testimonies and after some discussion, I expressed a willingness to embrace the Holy Spirit and the casting out of our demons. Master Kim prayed with us and called forth our demons. He allowed Jesus Christ to work through him to heal us just as Christ used his followers and disciples in the New Testament. While Master Kim prayed over me I felt something rising from within. Then, I felt a force on my right shoulder holding on to me and pulling me away. Eventually it stopped and I felt quite peaceful. My face was flush, yet I felt cool and comfortable.

Since that evening neither my hands nor my hips have had any pain.

Chapter V
God's Only "Way" of Escape

Learning how to get "connected" with God has a much more profound impact on our lives than just overcoming difficulty on earth. It is the very thing that will save your life for all eternity. Sound like a drastic statement? It is, and it's true. When we come into this world separated from God, and are never personally restored in a right relationship with God, we remain separated from Him, and under the power of Satan...forever! The sobering reality is that people who die spiritually "joined" with God spend eternity with God in heaven, and people who die spiritually connected with Satan, because of sin spend eternity with Satan in hell. Moreover, the condition of our spirits when we die is permanent! We are either saved from the punishment of our sin or condemned under the punishment of our sin. We either spend eternity in heaven or eternity in hell. There is no middle road.

Although many contend this information as nonsense, God disagrees. Hell is real. It is a real place with real fire. The Bible makes it clear this is a place of inconceivable pain and punishment. Not believing in hell will never stop you from going there. Jesus said to the disobedient and unbelieving...

> **"Then He will also say to those on the left hand, 'Depart from Me, you cursed, into the everlasting fire prepared for the devil and his angels...'" (Matthew 25:41)**

Know this above everything: We only pay the penalty of our sin *if* we refuse to accept the one true way God provided for our restoration and forgiveness. *Refusal to accept God's grace is to choose to be condemned!* People may delay and trivialize this eternal decision out of fear and deception, but it will never change the severity of consequence, which results from *refusing* to accept God's gift of forgiveness and eternal life.

There is nothing in all your life more important than finding truth and accepting the gift of God's grace. The difference between knowing and not knowing the truth is the difference between having eternal life in heaven and having eternal punishment in hell. You *must* find the "Way" to life, and then make a conscious decision to accept it. We either accept God's way of calling us back to Himself, and receive forgiveness of our sins, or we reject it. It cannot be stressed enough that there is *no* middle road.

> "See, I have set before you today life and good, death and evil, in that I command you today to love the Lord your God, to walk in His ways, and to keep His commandments, His statutes, and His judgements, that you may live and multiply; and the Lord your God will bless you in the land which you go to possess. But if your heart turns away so that you do not hear, and are drawn away, and worship other gods, and serve them, I announce to you today that you shall surely perish; you shall not prolong your days in the land which you cross over the Jordan to go in and possess. I call heaven and earth as witnesses today against you, that I have set before you life and death, blessing and cursing; therefore choose life, that both you and your descendants may live; that you may love the Lord your God, that you may obey His voice, and that you may cling to Him, for He is your life and the length of your days; and that you may dwell in the land which the Lord swore to your fathers, to Abraham, Isaac, and Jacob, to give them." (Deuteronomy 30:15–20)

> "He who believes in the Son has everlasting life; and he who does not believe the Son shall not see life, but the wrath of God abides on him." (John 3:36)

God's Grace and Love

It was never God's will or intention for His created children to be sent to hell and suffer eternal punishment. As discussed, God's will was to give us an abundant life with great blessing. God's love is so great toward us that He put a plan in motion for us to be forgiven and restored back to our original position as blessed children of God. God desires us to spend eternity with Him in Heaven, and this is why God has provided a way of escape from destruction!

> **"Even so it is not the will of your Father who is in heaven that one of these little ones should perish." (Matthew 18:14)**

Today, right now, each of us still has control of our will, and we still have the power to choose. We need to open our hearts, and see that God is calling us back to Himself today! He wants to draw you to Himself, and has prepared a way of forgiveness and mercy. God wants to give you not only the knowledge, but also the power and authority to conquer the strongholds in your life. He wants to give you 100 percent peace, health, and joy. It's His intense love for us that He has made this wonderful provision. It is our acceptance of His promise that will determine our success.

> **Do you not know that to whom you present yourselves slaves to obey, you are that one's slaves whom you obey, whether of sin leading to death, or of obedience leading to righteousness? (Romans 6:16)**

Debt Paid in Full

In order for God to restore us back to perfect union with Himself, He had to provide a way to deal with the enormous sin that separates us. This separation is so immense that no man or women could close the gap. God is the only one who could provide the "Way." People sometimes think they can do good deeds and live a good life to "earn" their way to heaven. Nothing could be further from the truth. We were all cursed to death through sin, and even our good works are unable to help since we still all fall short of the requirements of God's law.

The law expresses the righteousness of God, and proves the guilt of everyone since we have all broken God's law in some way. A brief look at the judgement of the United States legal system illustrates the severity of our sin. If a person lives most of their life as a law-abiding citizen, and one day in anger kills another person, they are deemed a murderer. Regardless of the good deeds they did before and after their crime, they are still guilty and required to pay for their own penalty with imprisonment or even their life! The justice of the court system in our democratic government still demands payment of the crime regardless of good deeds. We may think we are "good enough" in God's eyes, and never committed murder, but have you ever been angry with someone, hated someone, or been prideful? If yes, it's as if all the law had been broken.

> **For whoever shall keep the whole law, and yet stumble in one** *point*, **he is guilty of all. (James 2:10)**

> **...for all have sinned and fall short of the glory of God... (Romans 3:23)**

The sin debt is just too great for anyone to pay. Everyone is too guilty to get themselves out of their own sinful condition. This is why God needed to send someone to save us from destruction. This is why He sent His only begotten Son into the world, Jesus Christ. Jesus Christ was sent to pay our sin debt and provide a way to be forgiven. How? By trading His life for ours.

> **"For God so loved the world that He gave His only begotten Son, that whoever believes in Him should not perish but have everlasting life. For God did not send His Son into the world to condemn the world, but that the world through Him might be saved." (John 3:16–17)**

Can you imagine? God loves us so much that He sent His only Son, Jesus Christ, as a sacrifice to bear our punishment for all our sin from Adam until the end of the age! Yes, God sent Jesus Christ to die in our place and bear the penalty of our sin instead of us. He was willing to die the most painful death in history so that we could be completely free from the consequences of the fall in the Garden of Eden.

Christ has redeemed us from the curse of the law, having become a curse for us (for it is written, *"Cursed is everyone who hangs on a tree"*). (Galatians 3:13)

We must understand this incredible gift of grace. Grace means that God has bestowed something on us we really don't deserve. It is His gift of mercy and forgiveness.

If we are honest with ourselves, and with God, it is easy to admit we aren't perfect. We have missed the mark for what God has intended for us many, many, times. We are guilty and truly deserve the punishment for our sin. Thank God that He provided a way to be exonerated, a way for all of our wrongs to be erased, and a way for all of our mistakes to be forgiven.

This means everything you have ever done in your entire life no matter how bad or terrible will be forgiven because God's mercy is bigger, broader, and deeper than anything we can imagine. Read how Jesus Christ came like a second Adam to restore the relationship with our loving Father God.

For when we were still without strength, in due time Christ died for the ungodly. For scarcely for a righteous man will one die; yet perhaps for a good man someone would even dare to die. But God demonstrates His own love toward us, in that while we were still sinners, Christ died for us. Much more then, having now been justified by His blood, we shall be saved from wrath through Him. For if when we were enemies we were reconciled to God through the death of His Son, much more, having been reconciled, we shall be saved by His life. And not only that, but we also rejoice in God through our Lord Jesus Christ, through whom we have now received the reconciliation. Therefore, just as through one man sin entered the world, and death through sin, and thus death spread to all men, because all sinned—(For until the law sin was in the world, but sin is not imputed when there is no law. Nevertheless death reigned from Adam to Moses, even over those who had not sinned according to the likeness of the transgression of Adam, who is a type of Him who was to come. But the free gift is not like the offense. For if by the one man's offense many died, much more the grace of God and the gift by the grace of the one

Man, Jesus Christ, abounded to many. And the gift is not like that which came through the one who sinned. For the judgment which came from one offense resulted in condemnation, but the free gift which came from many offenses resulted in justification. For if by the one man's offense death reigned through the one, much more those who receive abundance of grace and of the gift of righteousness will reign in life through the One, Jesus Christ.) Therefore, as through one man's offense judgment came to all men, resulting in condemnation, even so through one Man's righteous act the free gift came to all men, resulting in justification of life. For as by one man's disobedience many were made sinners, so also by one Man's obedience many will be made righteous. Moreover the law entered that the offense might abound. But where sin abounded, grace abounded much more, so that as sin reigned in death, even so grace might reign through righteousness to eternal life through Jesus Christ our Lord. (Romans 5:6–21)

God has provided a free gift for us to be loosed from the devil's grip and from all sin and darkness in our lives. Jesus revealed God's plan to one of his servants:

"...to open their eyes, in order to turn them from darkness to light, and from the power of Satan to God, that they may receive forgiveness of sins and an inheritance among those who are sanctified by faith in Me." (Acts 26:18)

Only Jesus Christ can free us from sin because only He is perfect. He is God's Son. Every person born after Adam was made in the image and likeness of Adam tainted with sin. Trying to clean our own sin would be like cleaning something with a dirty rag...impossible! In contrast, Jesus Christ came not from man, but came directly from God. This is why He is without sin, and His blood is clean and spotless, able to make us clean.

In the days of ancient Israel, God's people offered perfect and unblemished animals as a sacrifice for payment for their sins. They brought the animal to the altar and shed its blood. The animal's blood was shed instead of theirs. In the same way, God our Father brought His unblemished (perfect) sacrifice for payment of *our* sins.

God's only Son, Jesus Christ, was perfect, sinless, and innocent. He gave His life for the guilty, and His blood was shed instead of ours, once, for all.

> **And He Himself is the propitiation for our sins, and not for ours only but also for the whole world. (1 John 2:2)**

How to Obtain God's Promise

THE ONE THING THAT GOD REQUIRES OF US TO BE FORGIVEN OF OUR SINS AND RECEIVE ETERNAL LIFE IS THAT WE BELIEVE JESUS CHRIST IS THE SON OF GOD WHO IS THE PAYMENT FOR OUR SIN.

> **For "whoever calls on the name of the LORD shall be saved." (Romans 10:13)**

God's promise says if we believe Jesus Christ is the Son of God who died for the forgiveness of our sins, we will be freed from the grip of Satan, and become children of God, inheriting eternal life! God's love provided a way for adoption so that we would no longer be connected to Satan in fear, but become blessed children of God.

> **For you did not receive the spirit of bondage again to fear, but you received the Spirit of adoption by whom we cry out, "Abba, Father." (Romans 8:15)**

Once we are united with God, we are changed into His likeness and become spiritually alive! We receive a new godly nature, and put to death the weaknesses and shortcomings of our old, "fallen nature." Yes! Putting your faith and trust in Jesus Christ will completely restore you to a "connected" relationship with God! God did not make it difficult to become His child. He is only looking for *your* freewill decision to choose life over death. All you have to do is grab hold of it with all your might!

> **But without faith it is impossible to please Him, for he who comes to God must believe that He is, and that He is a rewarder of those who diligently seek Him. (Hebrews 11:6)**

Despite the fact that many people still believe good works can "earn" their way to heaven, the *only* way is through faith in Jesus Christ. Being redeemed or freed from the curse of the Garden of Eden cannot happen with good deeds. It is the gift of God.

> **For by grace you have been saved through faith, and that not of yourselves; it is the gift of God, not of works, lest anyone should boast. (Ephesians 2:8–9)**

> **For the wages of sin *is* death, but the gift of God *is* eternal life in Christ Jesus our Lord. (Romans 6:23)**

In this next passage, we see one criminal who believed Jesus Christ was the Son of God, while the other criminal mocked Jesus and refused to believe. The man who believed was told that very day he would be with Jesus in Paradise. Jesus never spoke about limbo or purgatory, just Paradise. This man's faith is what saved his life. He did not have any time to get off his cross, do a bunch of good deeds, and then get back on his cross. No, it was his faith, and not deeds, that gave him entrance into Paradise.

> **Then one of the criminals who were hanged blasphemed Him, saying, "If you are the Christ, save Yourself and us." But the other, answering, rebuked him, saying, "Do you not even fear God, seeing you are under the same condemnation? And we indeed justly, for we receive the due reward of our deeds; but this Man has done nothing wrong." Then he said to Jesus, "Lord, remember me when You come into Your kingdom." And Jesus said to him, "Assuredly, I say to you, today you will be with Me in Paradise." (Luke 23:39–43)**

Good works cannot change our natures from being unholy to holy. They cannot change our natural desire for sin and bring life to our spirits. Though we call some people "good" because they have dedicated their lives to helping people, it doesn't necessarily mean their spirits have been made alive! Only God has the ability to do this! People with "dead" spirits (meaning without the life of God's spirit) do not reside with God and have no fellowship with Him. This is why our spirits must be made alive through faith in Jesus Christ for us to inherit eternal life.

The Bible tells the true story of a man named Nicodemus, a ruler of the Pharisees, and what most would call a very religious person. He was part of the strictest sect of the Jewish religion, and dedicated his life to following it. Most would think this man would have no problem entering heaven, but one thing was lacking.

Nicodemus knew there was something different about Jesus, and came to speak with Him. What Jesus said to him probably astounded him.

> **There was a man of the Pharisees named Nicodemus, a ruler of the Jews. This man came to Jesus by night and said to Him, "Rabbi, we know that You are a teacher come from God; for no one can do these signs that You do unless God is with him." Jesus answered and said to him, "Most assuredly, I say to you, unless one is born again, he cannot see the kingdom of God." (John 3:1–3)**

Jesus told Nicodemus that he needed to be transformed if he wanted to get into heaven. His spirit needed to be born again. The first time he was born, he was born in the likeness of Adam with a fallen, corrupt nature. Now Jesus told him that he must be born again with a new spiritual nature. He needed to be made new with the life of Christ. The same holds true for us!

> **Nicodemus said to Him, "How can a man be born when he is old? Can he enter a second time into his mother's womb and be born?" Jesus answered, "Most assuredly, I say to you, unless one is born of water and the Spirit, he cannot enter the kingdom of God. That which is born of the flesh is flesh, and that which is born of the Spirit is spirit." (John 3:4–6)**

Remember this is the same person many thought would have had no problem getting into Heaven! As you can see, breaking free from the devil and getting right with God are not achieved by performing good deeds. They're a matter of having our spiritual position changed from being a slave of Satan to a child of God through faith in Jesus Christ.

> **"For God did not send His Son into the world to condemn the world, but that the world through Him might be saved.**

> He who believes in Him is not condemned; but he who
> does not believe is condemned already, because he has not
> believed in the name of the only begotten Son of God."
> (John 3:17–18)

Do not be deceived by ceremony, tradition, or philosophy. God
teaches that Jesus Christ is the only "Way" to heaven.

> There is a way that seems right to a man, but its end is the
> way of death. (Proverbs 16:25)

> "Nor is there salvation in any other, for there is no other
> name under heaven given among men by which we must
> be saved." (Acts 4:12)

> Jesus said to him, "I am the way, the truth, and the life. No
> one comes to the Father except through Me." (John 14:6)

Having faith means putting your total trust in God's promise. It is a
conscious action of your will. Accept the gift to be free from Satan,
and put your faith in God's Son, Jesus Christ. Make Him the Lord
and Master of your life! Ask Jesus Christ to come into your life right
now! If you only go to church every Sunday and do charitable deeds
for the rest of your life, you will not be saved from hell. Even intellec-
tually knowing this information will not save you. You must accept it
with faith and meet Jesus Christ personally! Make a 100 percent com-
mitment to follow Him, and never turn back. This is the most important decision in your life. Don't wait until it is too late!

> Seek the Lord while He may be found, Call upon Him while
> He is near. Let the wicked forsake his way, And the unrigh-
> teous man his thoughts; Let him return to the Lord, And
> He will have mercy on him; And to our God, For He will
> abundantly pardon. (Isaiah 55:6–7)

> And He said to me, "It is done! I am the Alpha and the
> Omega, the Beginning and the End. I will give of the foun-
> tain of the water of life freely to him who thirsts. He who
> overcomes shall inherit all things and I will be his God
> and he shall be My son. But the cowardly, unbelieving, abomi-
> nable, murderers, sexually immoral, sorcerers, idolaters, and
> all liars shall have their part in the lake which burns with
> fire and brimstone, which is the second death." (Revela-
> tion 21:6–8)

Pray these words aloud to Jesus and He will come to you, and you will be saved. Open your heart. Ask Jesus to send His Holy Spirit to you. Believe, and you will be freed from the power of Satan and receive eternal life! This is God's promise!

> ...that if you confess with your mouth the Lord Jesus and believe in your heart that God has raised Him from the dead, you will be saved. For with the heart one believes unto righteousness, and with the mouth confession is made unto salvation. For the Scripture says, "Whoever believes on Him will not be put to shame." For there is no distinction between Jew and Greek, for the same Lord over all is rich to all who call upon Him. For "whoever calls on the name of the LORD shall be saved." (Romans 10:9–13)

Pray...

> Jesus, I realize I am a sinner and need to be forgiven of my sins. I no longer want to live my life separated from You. I believe that You are the Son of God, and that You died so that I can be forgiven of my sins. I accept You as my personal Savior and turn away from my sin. I want to go forward trusting You as the Lord of my life, and will follow you all my days. Please save me, and send Your Holy Spirit to me! I ask this in the name of Jesus Christ. Amen.

When you prayed these words, and meant it with all of your heart, you have become a child of God! You have been freed from Satan and have been given a new life! You are no longer under the curse! You are free!

> And you He made alive, who were dead in trespasses and sins, in which you once walked according to the course of this world, according to the prince of the power of the air, the spirit who now works in the sons of disobedience, among whom also we all once conducted ourselves in the lusts of our flesh, fulfilling the desires of the flesh and of the mind, and were by nature children of wrath, just as the others. But God, who is rich in mercy, because of His great love with which He loved us, even when we were dead in trespasses, made us alive together with Christ (by grace you

have been saved), and raised us up together, and made us sit together in the heavenly places in Christ Jesus, that in the ages to come He might show the exceeding riches of His grace in his kindness toward us in Christ Jesus. For by grace you have been saved through faith, and that not of yourselves; it is the gift of God, not of works, lest anyone should boast. For we are His workmanship, created in Christ Jesus for good works, which God prepared beforehand that we should walk in them. (Ephesians 2:1–10)

Record today's date and never forget it because today is your spiritual birthday! Today is the beginning of the rest of your life! You are now a child of God able to receive every blessing that God has provided you. You can now stand in God's promise to overcome all sickness, disease, trouble, and all the power of the enemy. You are no longer a slave to the trouble in your life! You are free! Read on to learn how to make God's promise a reality in your life.

TESTIMONY: Carol Cornacchia
Birth Date: June 17, 1964
Occupation: Export Services Specialist
Experience: **Healed from a pulled muscle**
Date of Testimony: Not Recorded

I took a Tae Kwon Do class and the next day, I took a kickboxing class. In the kickboxing class I did not stretch well. When I did a sidekick, I actually heard and felt that I pulled something in my leg. It hurt me for months. I tried heat, Advil, and ice, but it still hurt. In one class, we were doing kicks, and suddenly I felt tears coming down my cheeks. I was in so much pain! Master Kim asked me to see him about the pain in my leg. That night we read from the Bible and he discussed heaven and hell with me. Everything started to make sense. We continued reading the Bible. He advised that the evil demons are looking for a house (body) to live in. We need to get them out—I am God's daughter. As he was talking, my body started to shiver. I was not cold, but I was shaking. I was told that the reason I was shivering was because the demons did not like what we were reading or talking about (God). We continued to pray. Master Kim told the demons to get out and I just fell to the ground. After all that was done I was so tired. My husband said my face looked like it was glowing. I did not feel pain at all in my leg. I was amazed! Even during and after the workout, my leg was fine. I thank God for this. I am still struggling with more problems (that are personal), but I know that God is there. If I need help, I can rely on Jesus to be there and to keep my faith strong.

Chapter VI
Victory: God's Promise in Jesus Christ

Many people are aware that Jesus Christ had nails driven through His hands and feet, was hung on a cross, and died for the forgiveness of sins. However, many are completely unaware that Jesus Christ has also provided the power to overcome all forms of sickness, disease, weakness, and trouble. This is why so many believers still suffer with troubles just the same as those who do not yet know Jesus Christ as their personal Savior. This is why we need to study God's word more closely concerning the promises of God through Jesus Christ.

The Deliverer

As we have discussed, Jesus Christ was sent to earth to provide much more than morality. Jesus Christ came to earth to provide a way of salvation and to destroy the works of the devil. This is why Jesus Christ is rightly called our Deliverer. To "deliver" means to rescue from imminent danger when someone or something attacks. To illustrate, picture yourself on a battlefield with the enemy looking straight into your eyes about to strike you with a sword. At the last moment, someone destroys the enemy saving your life in the nick of time. In our lives, the spiritual world is the battlefield. The attacker is Satan, and the deliverer is Jesus Christ. We must

48

understand that Jesus Christ did not come to save the earth or to bring peace to the world. He came to rescue us from it and destroy the works of the devil. Jesus Himself said,

> "Do not think that I came to bring peace on earth. I did not come to bring peace but a sword." (Matthew 10:34)

> ...For this purpose the Son of God was manifested, that He might destroy the works of the devil. (1 John 3:8)

Here we explicitly see that Jesus destroyed the power of Satan, and freed those who were in bondage to him!

> Inasmuch then as the children have partaken of flesh and blood, He Himself likewise shared in the same, that through death He might destroy him who had the power of death, that is, the devil, and release those who through fear of death were all their lifetime subject to bondage. (Hebrews 2:14)

We even see this purpose was already determined and planned in Genesis during God's judgement of Satan. God spoke to Satan,

> "...He shall bruise your head, and you shall bruise His heel." (Genesis 3:15)

The first "He" refers to Jesus Christ bruising Satan's head (a vital spot that would bring destruction). The second part refers to Satan bruising the heel of Jesus Christ (a nonvital spot), which refers to His crucifixion. In other words, although "you" (Satan) will make your attempt to destroy Jesus Christ, "He" will not be overcome and will destroy you forever. Jesus even made a public spectacle of the enemy.

> Having disarmed principalities and power, He made a public spectacle of them, triumphing over them in it. (Colossians 2:15)

Death could not hold Jesus, and He rose from the grave on the third day.

> "Him, being delivered by the determined purpose and foreknowledge of God, you have taken by lawless hands, have

crucified, and put to death; whom God raised up, having
loosed the pains of death, because it was not possible that
He should be held by it." (Acts 2:23–24)

"By His Stripes We Are Healed"

To further understand the effect of Jesus Christ's sacrifice, let's
look at the prophecy of Isaiah in the Old Testament (written before
Jesus physically came to earth). It reveals God's promise to us about
the pain and suffering you may be dealing with right now. It is a
promise that can never and will never be taken away.

> Who has believed our report? And to whom has the arm of
> the Lord been revealed? For He shall grow up before Him
> as a tender plant, And as a root out of dry ground. He has
> no form or comeliness; And when we see Him, There is no
> beauty that we should desire Him. He is despised and re-
> jected by men, A Man of sorrows and acquainted with grief.
> And we hid, as it were, our faces from Him; He was de-
> spised, And we did not esteem Him. Surely He has borne
> our griefs And carried our sorrows; yet we esteemed Him
> stricken, Smitten by God, and afflicted. But He was
> wounded for our transgressions, He was bruised for our
> iniquities; The chastisement for our peace was upon Him,
> And by His stripes we are healed. All we like sheep have
> gone astray; We have turned, everyone, to his own way;
> And the Lord has laid on Him the iniquity of us all. (Isaiah
> 53:1–6)

This passage reveals crucial detail concerning the blessing we
receive from Jesus' sacrifice. Isaiah describes Jesus coming to the
earth with no special glamour or theatrics. In fact, Jesus had no
beauty or any special characteristics that would make people interested in Him. He was even despised and rejected by men, and frequently acquainted with grief! Why would God subject His only
Son to this life of pain and suffering, only to end it in an excruciat-
ingly painful death? The reason is Jesus Christ took all the pain,
suffering, and punishment that was meant for us in order to pay the
penalty for *our* sins.

Verse four of the passage in Isaiah says that Jesus Christ "has borne our griefs" (in Hebrew *griefs* is *choliy* translated *sicknesses*) and carried our sorrows (in Hebrew *sorrows* is *makobah* translated *pains*). It then goes on to say that He was wounded for our transgressions (in Hebrew *transgression* is *pesha* meaning sin), and that He was bruised for our weaknesses. The punishment for our peace was also upon Him! It is so important to understand the depth of pain that Jesus Christ had to go through to pay our sin debt. He endured more pain in His mind and body than anybody ever has or will, and He willingly did it because of His love for us!

The next part reveals the promise. Because Jesus suffered for every one of us, *"We...are healed."* Yes! Jesus Christ accepted all the punishment for our sins, and ended the curse in the Garden of Eden for those who believe in Him!

Look at what Jesus did...

1. He took *our* pains.
2. He took *our* sicknesses.
3. He was wounded for *our* sin.
4. He was bruised for *our* weaknesses.
5. He accepted the punishment for *our* peace.

} **The result: "...we are healed!"**

This makes perfect sense. If Jesus took all of our sufferings and pains, we shouldn't keep them! Jesus has restored our relationship with God, destroyed the works of the devil, and as we will soon discuss, has given us power and authority to stand strong in His promises. God clearly does not want you to be weak and sick. If He did, He never would have sent His only Son to suffer so much pain to take it away! We also know it is God's will to heal us 100 percent because we see Isaiah's prophecy come true!

> Now when Jesus had come into Peter's house, He saw his wife's mother lying sick with a fever. So He touched her hand, and the fever left her. And she arose and served them. When evening had come, they brought to Him many who were demon-possessed. And He cast out the spirits with a word, and healed all who were sick, that it might be

fulfilled which was spoken by Isaiah the prophet, saying: "He Himself took our infirmities and bore our sicknesses." (Matthew 8:14–17)

Jesus came and saw a common, everyday situation...a woman with a fever. However, unlike anyone in history, Jesus not only wanted her to be well, he had the power to make her well. So *"He touched her hand, and the fever left her."* (Matthew 8:15) Then He saw many people in the village sick. He immediately took action by casting out the demons in their bodies so they would be healed. Isaiah is not just talking about our spiritual healing, although that is a great part of it. He is describing healing that fully encompasses our minds, bodies, and spirits. We know this is true because Jesus clearly healed Peter's mother-in-law's body, and many others who were physically sick.

It is unfortunate that many people believe the promises and blessings of God are only experienced after we die. The blessings of being a Christian start immediately upon accepting Jesus Christ as your personal Savior, right now here on earth! Many Christians have become so rooted in religious tradition and philosophy they have forgotten the great promises of God are actually true! We have grown to accept our pains, weaknesses, and sicknesses as part of life. This is one of Satan's greatest deceptions. He gets our expectation levels so low that we come to expect nothing of what God has already provided through the sacrifice of His Son Jesus Christ. This is why Satan is called the "thief." (John 10:10)

There are many other Christians who believe that God's promises are true, but never act on them. This too comes from great deception. God is alive, and is a God of action. This means He wants you to take action in your life, and not just have knowledge in your mind. God wants His children to stand up and take hold of all of His blessings. We must be doers of His Word, and not just hearers of His word.

But be doers of the word, and not hearers only, deceiving yourselves. (James 1:22)

We must be alert and determined to receive all that Jesus has promised, and we must keep in mind that Jesus came to bring an abundant life while Satan aims to bring only harm and destruction.

> **"The thief does not come except to steal, and to kill, and to destroy. I have come that they may have life, and that they may have it more abundantly." (John 10:10)**

TESTIMONY: Abraham Gablanco
Birth Date: February 27, 1963
Occupation: Mechanic
Experience: **Healed from a shoulder injury**
Date of Testimony: April 4, 1995

When I first started attending Blue Dragon Tae Kwon Do Academy back in August 1992 I suffered from intense pain and impeded movement in my left shoulder. Master Kim, during my daily workout, noticed I was having problems with my shoulder. After a few days Master Kim approached me and asked me what was wrong. I told him about the pain and difficulty I was having. That same day after class, Master Kim took me to his office where he prayed for me intensely and removed the demons from my body. Since that day, thanks to God, my shoulder is 100 percent improved and I have total movement in my left shoulder.

Chapter VII
The Spiritual World

Many acknowledge another world exists beyond our physical realm, but very little is understood about it. We so commonly hear and see the media present such things as ghosts, evil spirits, Ouija boards, seances, fortune-telling, and witchcraft that we have lost sight of the true nature of these things. There was a time when people easily discerned the difference between good and evil, but our modern world has merged these elements leaving people ignorant of the enormous danger existing in the spiritual realm. Sadly, many Christian churches avoid discussion of the spiritual world fearing it may cause offense and uneasiness. This leaves most completely unaware of how these spiritual things fit into Christianity, and how these forces impact our daily lives.

In contrast, the Bible explicitly teaches that we need to be armed with an expert understanding of the spiritual world if we are to live in the blessing that God has provided. Think of it. Of all the knowledge in all creation that God could have given us in the Bible, He determined to teach us the workings of the spiritual world. Truly, God does not want us to be ignorant of this world!

> ...lest Satan should take advantage of us; for we are not ignorant of his devices. (2 Corinthians 2:11)

The Battle Is Spiritual, Not Physical

It would be great if all our problems instantly vanished when we accepted Jesus Christ into our hearts, but this obviously isn't the case. This is why it is imperative we understand that although we live in a physical environment, we are in the midst of an enormous spiritual struggle. Despite this reality, many people are still unaware and confused as to why their lives don't automatically get easier. We ask, "If I am a child of God, why do I still have all this difficulty in my life?" The answer lies in the fact that although our spiritual natures have been made new, our physical bodies still reside in this world where the devil is working.

Christians are not exempt from temptation, sickness, disease, or any other problem in life. If you doubt this, take a look at other Christians you know and see if any of them live trouble-free. What problem comes to a non-Christian that doesn't also come to a Christian? You're right, there aren't any! We are all challenged with the same exact difficulties. The great difference between someone who has Jesus Christ in their heart, and someone who doesn't, is that Christians are made more than conquerors over all the power of the enemy. Yes, trouble will still come, but if you have Jesus Christ, you are enabled to overcome it! Read the following verses and understand that although we live in this world, we are not overcome by this world because of Jesus!

> What then shall we say to these things? If God is for us, who can be against us? He who did not spare His own Son, but delivered Him up for us all, how shall He not with Him also freely give us all things? Who shall bring a charge against God's elect? It is God who justifies. Who is he who condemns? It is Christ who died, and furthermore is also risen, who is even at the right hand of God, who also makes intercession for us. Who shall separate us from the love of Christ? Shall tribulation, or distress, or persecution, or famine, or nakedness, or peril, or sword? As it is written: "For Your sake we are killed all day long; We are accounted as sheep for the slaughter." Yet in all these things we are more than conquerors through Him who loved us. (Romans 8:31–37)

"I do not pray that You should take them out of the world, but that You should keep them from the evil one." (John 17:15)

"These things I have spoken to you, that in Me you may have peace. In the world you will have tribulation; but be of good cheer, I have overcome the world." (John 16:33)

The critical point is to understand that our struggles take place in the spiritual realm, and not in the physical realm. This is why it is critical to understand how to stand strong in the power and might of Jesus Christ so we may become victorious in *every* situation.

For though we walk in the flesh, we do not war according to the flesh. For the weapons of our warfare are not carnal but mighty in God for pulling down strongholds, casting down arguments and every high thing that exalts itself against the knowledge of God, bringing every thought into captivity to the obedience of Christ... (2 Corinthians 10:3–5)

This knowledge can easily make us feel uncomfortable because we are so accustomed to living by what we see, feel, hear, taste, and touch. We have for so long been trained to rely only on our five senses that we are not immediately confident resisting something we cannot see, hear, or even measure. This is why many only know about the spiritual world from a distance, but still battle their trouble according to physical principles. This focus on the physical world makes it difficult to receive the complete blessings of God, and often leads to discouragement. Thank God that He has not left us ignorant of the true spiritual nature of our problems, and reveals how to resist and overcome the devil's tactics. Read the following verses about this spiritual battle, and make a decision to no longer resist with physical means only. Strive to resist the devil with spiritual means. Read the call to action to prepare for spiritual warfare.

Finally, my brethren, be strong in the Lord and in the power of His might. Put on the whole armor of God, that you may be able to stand against the wiles of the devil. For we do not wrestle against flesh and blood, but against principalities, against powers, against the rulers of the darkness of this age, against spiritual hosts of wickedness in the heavenly places. Therefore take up the whole armor of God, that you may be able to withstand in the evil day, and having done all, to stand. Stand therefore, having girded your waist with truth, having put on the breastplate of righteousness, and having shod your feet with the preparation of the gospel of peace; above all, taking the shield of faith with which you will be able to quench all the fiery darts of the wicked one. And take the helmet of salvation, and the sword of the Spirit, which is the word of God; praying always with all prayer and supplication in the Spirit, being watchful to this end with all perseverance and supplication for all the saints... (Ephesians 6:10–18)

Did you see it?

For we do not wrestle against flesh and blood, but against principalities, against powers, against the rulers of the darkness of this age, against spiritual hosts of wickedness in the heavenly places. (Ephesians 6:12)

This means the devil has a well-organized, hierarchical army in place. When one-third of the angels were cast out of heaven and sent to the earth, (Revelation 12:9) they immediately fell under the devil's control and began working towards his goal to kill, steal, and destroy. This is why we wrestle *"against principalities, against powers, against the rulers of the darkness of this age, against spiritual hosts of wickedness in the heavenly places."* (Ephesians 6:12) Satan knows he cannot do as much damage to God's kingdom by himself so he mobilizes these "principalities" and "rulers of darkness" into an army to "eat" the dust or "flesh" of mankind. (Genesis 3:14)

Realizing we are in the midst of a spiritual war with Satan and his army, let's better understand these principalities and powers so you can overcome the root of your troubles.

How Satan Causes Destruction

Although critical, it is not at all sufficient to simply understand Satan is looking to destroy us. We must explore the word of God

deeper to uncover the workings of how our minds and bodies become sick and diseased. Please let us explain that this information
may be a little unnerving at first, but remember: You are a child of
God and the enemy no longer has any power over you. God will
always protect you from evil, no matter what, God is your refuge,
and nothing can overcome Him!

> **But the Lord is faithful, who will establish you and guard**
> **you from the evil one. (2 Thessalonians 3:3)**

Let's explore how the Bible shows Jesus Christ delivered the
sick and oppressed.

> **As they went out, behold, they brought to Him a man, mute**
> **and demon-possessed. And when the demon was cast out,**
> **the mute spoke. And the multitudes marveled, saying, "It**
> **was never seen like this in Israel!" (Matthew 9:32–33)**

In this passage, people brought to Jesus a man who couldn't speak.
The Bible doesn't go into detail about the physical reasons why the
man's larynx didn't work. The Bible gives a more accurate diagno-
sis of the sickness: a demon was inside of his body! At first glance, it
may appear that he has two problems. One was that he was mute,
and the other was that he was demon-possessed. We know this is
not the case because we see that when the demon was cast out, the
mute spoke! The sickness and the demon were one and the same!
Jesus knowing this information performed only *one* necessary action. He got rid of, or "cast out," the demon. The Bible then tells us
the mute spoke! This is a clear cause-and-effect relationship. Many
erroneously believe that demon possession is separate from sickness and disease. Our modern society may try to separate the physical from the spiritual, but they are inextricably linked! When Jesus
cast out the mute demon, the problem left, and the man spoke! This
makes perfect sense. The devil and his army are the agents of suffering and pain. Remove them and you remove the cause of the
pain! This is exactly what Jesus did. No one in all of history had this
kind of authority to command evil spirits to leave. This is why those

who witnessed His act said, *"It was never seen like this in Israel!"* (Matthew 9:33)

The spiritual world is much bigger and more powerful than the physical world. Physical laws of nature do not apply. For example, in the physical world, two objects cannot occupy the same space, but they can in the spiritual world. This is why it is possible for an evil spirit to get inside of a person's body.

Please understand this is not anything like Hollywood's portrayal of demons. When most people think of a demon being inside someone, they think of a dramatic and extremely obvious experience. Satan is much craftier than he would have you believe. Demons enter people without theatrics and special effects. It usually happens without people ever noticing or feeling it in any way. We only witness the symptoms, or signs, of the problem, such as high blood pressure, migraines, cancer, heart disease, lupus, allergies, infections, psychological problems, etc.

The Bible consistently teaches us to look deeper, past physical symptoms into the spiritual root. If it were necessary to teach us about the human anatomy to overcome disease, God would have done it. The fact is...He didn't. Instead, God taught us the root of sickness in the spiritual world. Why would it be necessary for Jesus Christ to suffer so much pain and destroy Satan's power if the root of sickness was physical? Why would we be healed by His stripes if our problems had nothing to do with spiritual enemies, and everything to do with bacteria and viruses? God could have just let us work it out ourselves with modern medicine. The fact is that He didn't because God dealt with the real problem in the world: principalities, powers, and rulers of the darkness of this age. You no longer need to wonder where you got your trouble from, or what caused it. Now you know it is not so much "what" is bothering you, but rather "who" is bothering you.

Let's look at some other examples from the Bible to further validate this information.

Now He was teaching in one of the synagogues on the Sabbath. And behold, there was a woman who had a spirit of infirmity eighteen years, and was bent over and could in

> no way raise herself up. But when Jesus saw her, He called
> her to Him and said to her, "Woman, you are loosed from
> your infirmity." And He laid His hands on her, and imme-
> diately she was made straight, and glorified God. But the
> ruler of the synagogue answered with indignation, because
> Jesus had healed on the Sabbath; and he said to the crowd,
> "There are six days on which men ought to work; therefore
> come and be healed on them, and not on the Sabbath day."
> The Lord then answered him and said, "Hypocrite! Does
> not each one of you on the Sabbath loose his ox or donkey
> from the stall, and lead it away to water it? So ought not
> this woman, being a daughter of Abraham, whom Satan
> has bound—think of it—for eighteen years, be loosed from
> this bond on the Sabbath?" (Luke 13:10–16)

Here we see a common occurrence. A woman is hunched over
and cannot stand up straight. Most of us would probably think her
condition is a natural part of growing old, but Jesus, knowing everything, knew better. He diagnosed her as having a *"spirit of infirmity"* for 18 years! After He called her to Himself, He freed her from
the infirmity, and she was immediately made straight. There is no
other conclusion to draw about the cause of sickness other than a
spiritual enemy. Jesus even explicitly says that Satan had bound her
for 18 years.

> "So ought not this woman, being a daughter of Abraham,
> whom Satan has bound—think of it—for eighteen years,
> be loosed from this bond on the Sabbath?" (Luke 13:16)

We have gotten so caught up in our intellectual, scientific research
that we have completely lost focus of what God our Father has so
clearly taught us in the Bible. Here is another example of a man
who, for a lack of a better word, went insane and met Jesus face to
face.

> Then they came to the other side of the sea, to the country
> of the Gadarenes. And when He had come out of the boat,
> immediately there met Him out of the tombs a man with
> an unclean spirit, who had his dwelling among the tombs;
> and no one could bind him, not even with chains, because
> he had often been bound with shackles and chains. And

the chains had been pulled apart by him, and the shackles broken in pieces; neither could anyone tame him. And always, night and day, he was in the mountains and in the tombs, crying out and cutting himself with stones. When he saw Jesus from afar, he ran and worshiped Him. And he cried out with a loud voice and said, "What have I to do with You, Jesus, Son of the Most High God? I implore You by God that You do not torment me." For He said to him, "Come out of the man, unclean spirit!" Then He asked him, "What is your name?" And he answered, saying, "My name is Legion; for we are many." Also he begged Him earnestly that He would not send them out of the country. Now a large herd of swine was feeding there near the mountains. So all the demons begged Him, saying, "Send us to the swine, that we may enter them." And at once Jesus gave them permission. Then the unclean spirits went out and entered the swine (there were about two thousand); and the herd ran violently down the steep place into the sea, and drowned in the sea. So those who fed the swine fled, and they told it in the city and in the country. And they went out to see what it was that had happened. Then they came to Jesus, and saw the one who had been demon-possessed and had the legion, sitting and clothed and in his right mind. And they were afraid. And those who saw it told them how it happened to him who had been demon-possessed, and about the swine. Then they began to plead with Him to depart from their region. And when He got into the boat, he who had been demon-possessed begged Him that he might be with Him. However, Jesus did not permit him, but said to him, "Go home to your friends, and tell them what great things the Lord has done for you, and how He has had compassion on you." And he departed and began to proclaim in Decapolis all that Jesus had done for him; and all marveled. (Mark 5:1–20)

This is exactly the kind of person we would find in a mental hospital treated with medication. Again, the Bible diagnoses the man's problem as being caused by evil spirits, and *not* caused by chemical imbalances. This man was being held as a slave by the devil, and Jesus freed him by casting the unclean spirits out with a command. The effect: the one who had been demon-possessed by the legion of demons was "sitting and clothed and in his right mind"! He completely and immediately recovered! Can you see the clarity of the Bible? We could spend countless years trying to figure out the complexity of the human mind. We could even spend millions of dollars to develop medications to treat the mind, but would still miss the root cause because it's spiritual, and not physical! Despite the fact that symptoms may differ, the root cause and treatment remain the same.

These bystanders clearly witnessed the effect of these unclean spirits when Jesus sent them into the herd of pigs. It is common knowledge that pigs don't naturally commit suicide, but they did that day because evil spirits entered them. People also are not naturally prone to suicide, but are victims of the same evil root.

Let's look at another example where evil spirits caused sickness in the human body.

> **And when they had come to the multitude, a man came to Him, kneeling down to Him and saying, "Lord, have mercy on my son, for he is an epileptic and suffers severely; for he often falls into the fire and often into the water. So I brought him to Your disciples, but they could not cure him." Then Jesus answered and said, "O faithless and perverse generation, how long shall I be with you? How long shall I bear with you? Bring him here to Me." And Jesus rebuked the demon, and it came out of him; and the child was cured from that very hour. Then the disciples came to Jesus privately and said, "Why could we not cast it out?" So Jesus said to them, "Because of your unbelief; for assuredly, I say to you, if you have faith as a mustard seed, you will say to this mountain, 'Move from here to there,' and it will move; and nothing will be impossible for you. However, this kind does not go out except by prayer and fasting." (Matthew 17:14–21)**

In this situation, we see a boy who has epilepsy, a condition typically manifested by convulsive attacks. Even though there is a different physical manifestation, Jesus still diagnosed the boy as having a demon. He cast out the demon with a command, and the boy was made well. Even though the boy's father said he had epilepsy, Jesus saw past the symptom straight to the root and removed it. Again, it is simple cause-and-effect relationship.

> **When evening had come, they brought to Him many who were demon-possessed. And He cast out the spirits with a word, and healed all who were sick... (Matthew 8:16)**

> **And He was casting out a demon, and it was mute. So it was, when the demon had gone out, that the mute spoke; and the multitudes marveled. (Luke 11:14)**

All sickness is a form of oppression, and understanding the cause is a great step toward allowing Jesus to remove it! The critical key to understand is that Jesus freed these people from their maladies by removing the presence of evil in their bodies. If Jesus healed those who were oppressed by the devil, then it means He will do the same thing for you and me today.

Imagine if a relative left a large inheritance to you in their will. The money is yours, but you still have to use the key they gave you to open the safe and get the money. If not, the money will remain in the safe, and you will remain without the blessing. In the same way, this knowledge is a sort of key to help understand how to overcome our problems.

It is important to note that not every account of healing mentions evil behind the sickness. Each account of healing teaches and demonstrates a different aspect of knowledge. Not every healing account focuses on the cause of the sickness. Some show the reason the people were healed, while some show why they weren't. Still others show the proper attitude toward God's word and resulting grace. Scripture always teaches scripture, and every account of healing perfectly fits together equipping us with a complete understanding of how to overcome.

In the next chapter, we will discuss in greater detail that Jesus Christ wants us to be healed no matter what the sickness or problem.

> **"...how God anointed Jesus of Nazareth with the Holy Spirit and with power, who went about doing good and healing all who were oppressed by the devil, for God was with Him." (Acts 10:38)**

TESTIMONY: Bob Shadowski
Birth Date: December 21, 1988
Occupation: Student
Experience: **Healed from hearing defect and asthma**
Date of Testimony: January 15, 1998

Since I was born I had a lot of problems. I was born with an ear problem and just recently got asthma. I always had a lot of problems in school or at home with the illnesses. I would sometimes go to school and have the nurse call home saying I wasn't feeling well. At night I wouldn't be able to sleep and my ear would hurt. I went to doctors and they said that all of it was just minor. They gave me tablets that I would have to take everyday. When I joined Blue Dragon Tae Kwon Do Academy, Master Kim saw me struggling. He asked me what the problem was. I told him, and he said that my disease could be cured. That night my mother and I went to see Master Kim. He asked me to read out of the Bible. We read and as we went along he explained everything to us. As he explained everything to us there would be an example of it in the Bible. Then I knew God was going to cure me. After reading out of the Bible, he prayed for me and during that time I felt a slight breeze blow in the room. Master Kim allowed Jesus Christ to use him to get my evil spirit out of my body. After he had finished praying I had felt a little better. I've been praying ever since and my problems are gone. My ears don't bother me. My asthma doesn't affect me, and I feel great. I'd like to thank God and Jesus for curing me, and I believe He could help others.

Chapter VIII

Jesus Wants *You* to Overcome!

It can sometimes be difficult to fully understand the vastness of God's love for us. We are sometimes so riddled with guilt, fear, and poor self-worth that we do not feel worthy of God's love. These feelings leave us thinking, "Jesus healed other people but that doesn't mean He will heal me." We think, "Maybe Jesus wants me to suffer with this particular illness. Maybe Jesus isn't going to hear my prayer, or maybe it's not God's will for me to be healed. I just don't deserve it."

It is true that none of us deserves to be blessed, but thank God that He has not given us what we deserve! We deserve punishment, but God has given grace instead! He wants us to live in the fullness of His joy and dwell in the greatness of His mercy. We all must wake up and realize that we are not lowly creations in this world. We are handmade creations of God Almighty. We are sons and daughters of the *King of Kings and Lord of Lords* (Revelation 19:16) who have been redeemed by God and given back our position as His sons and daughters. You must grasp how much you are worth in God's eyes! You must understand God wants to pour out His love for you more abundantly than you can imagine. Look at the potential of what God can do if only we would believe!

Now to Him who is able to do exceedingly abundantly above all that we ask or think, according to the power that works in us. (Ephesians 3:20)

Yes, God wants to accomplish more in us than we can even ask or think! Ironically, it is our own attitude that often limits God from working in our lives rather than God holding us back! Think of it, the Bible says,

> **...being confident of this very thing, that He who has begun a good work in you will complete it until the day of Jesus Christ... (Philippians 1:6)**

This knowledge alone should give you the confidence to approach God with expectation of deliverance from every trial and tribulation. When you fully understand the vastness of God's love, your doubts about His willingness to heal you will be dispelled.

We can get a glimpse of God's feeling toward us when we're sick if we consider a parent's reaction to his or her sick child. At the first sign of a problem, parents move into action to ensure they do all they can to make their children feel better. Parents frequently state they wish they could somehow suffer with the sickness instead of their children. In fact my own mother, when I was diagnosed with cancer, said she wished she could take the cancer instead of me. That is the kind of love that God showed us through His Son Jesus Christ. The difference is Jesus not only had the will to take sickness and disease from us, He also had the power. Jesus Christ died for everyone's sin, everyone's sickness, and everyone's pain! No one is outside His love! God loves each and every one of us with the same kind of passion and shows no favoritism.

> **For there is no partiality with God. (Romans 2:11)**

Jesus Christ wants to heal us of *all* pain, and isn't selective with the type of pain or disease. The Bible clearly says,

> **"...how God anointed Jesus of Nazareth with the Holy Spirit and with power, who went about doing good and healing all who were oppressed by the devil, for God was with Him." (Acts 10:38)**

> **Then Jesus went about all the cities and villages, teaching in their synagogues, preaching the gospel of the kingdom,**

and healing every sickness and every disease among the people. (Matthew 9:35)

Jesus went *"healing every sickness and every disease among the people."* Jesus never selected the types of diseases He wanted to heal. Even parents don't reason in their hearts to keep one type of pain in their children, while they want another type of pain to leave. Thank God we don't have to wonder if we have the one disease Jesus is unwilling to heal—every sickness, every disease, and every problem are covered by the blood of Jesus Christ's sacrifice!

And behold, a leper came and worshiped Him, saying, "Lord, if You are willing, You can make me clean." Then Jesus put out His hand and touched him, saying, "I am willing; be cleansed." Immediately his leprosy was cleansed. And Jesus said to him, "See that you tell no one; but go your way, show yourself to the priest, and offer the gift that Moses commanded, as a testimony to them." (Matthew 8:2–4)

This is such a wonderful passage! So many people pray, "Lord, if it is your will, please heal me." This leper asked the same question as we do today. Face to face, the leper asked Jesus whether it was His will to heal him. Jesus answered him with the clearest answer possible, *"I am willing; be cleansed."* At that moment, the leper was healed! Jesus' response to this man's question was placed in the scripture for our learning! Do not miss God's blessing by doubting that it is His will for you to be healed. Jesus' answer is emphatically *"I am willing."* We don't need to wonder any longer.

And when Jesus went out He saw a great multitude; and He was moved with compassion for them, and healed their sick. (Matthew 14:14)

Now as they went out of Jericho, a great multitude followed Him. And behold, two blind men sitting by the road, when they heard that Jesus was passing by, cried out, saying, "Have mercy on us, O Lord, Son of David!" Then the multitude warned them that they should be quiet; but they cried out all the more, saying, "Have mercy on us, O Lord,

> Son of David!" So Jesus stood still and called them, and
> said, "What do you want Me to do for you?" They said to
> Him, "Lord, that our eyes may be opened." So Jesus had
> compassion and touched their eyes. And immediately their
> eyes received sight, and they followed Him. (Matthew
> 20:29–34)

In the example mentioned above, we see Jesus was moved with
compassion for their need, and responded by healing the sick. Jesus
is still moved with compassion when we cry out to Him for deliverance from our trouble.

> Then one of the crowd answered and said, "Teacher, I
> brought You my son, who has a mute spirit. And wherever
> it seizes him, it throws him down; he foams at the mouth,
> gnashes his teeth, and becomes rigid. So I spoke to Your
> disciples, that they should cast it out, but they could not."
> He answered him and said, "O faithless generation, how
> long shall I be with you? How long shall I bear with you?
> Bring him to Me." Then they brought him to Him. And
> when he saw Him, immediately the spirit convulsed him,
> and he fell on the ground and wallowed, foaming at the
> mouth. So He asked his father, "How long has this been
> happening to him?"
> And he said, "From childhood. And often he has thrown
> him both into the fire and into the water to destroy him.
> But if You can do anything, have compassion on us and
> help us." Jesus said to him, "If you can believe, all things
> are possible to him who believes." Immediately the father
> of the child cried out and said with tears, "Lord, I believe;
> help my unbelief!" When Jesus saw that the people came
> running together, He rebuked the unclean spirit, saying to
> it, "Deaf and dumb spirit, I command you, come out of him
> and enter him no more!" Then the spirit cried out, convulsed
> him greatly, and came out of him. And he became as one
> dead, so that many said, "He is dead." But Jesus took him
> by the hand and lifted him up, and he arose. (Mark 9:17–27)

Here a boy had a mute demon, and Jesus' disciples, those closest to Him, tried to pray for the boy so he would be healed. The boy
wasn't. Our logic may dictate that if the disciples prayed, and they

were closest to Jesus, then it must not be God's will for the boy to be healed. It sounds like a reasonable argument because this is exactly what happens today. We pray for someone who is sick, and nothing happens. We quickly conclude that it wasn't God's will to heal the person. We could not be further from the truth! When Jesus was confronted with this situation, He immediately made a comment that shocks many people. He said, *"O faithless and perverse generation, how long shall I be with you?"* Jesus then rebuked the demon, and it came out and the boy was healed. It was absolutely God's will for the boy to be healed because Jesus healed him! The reason the disciples could not heal the boy is found in Mark, verse 19.

> **He answered him and said, "O faithless generation, how long shall I be with you? How long shall I bear with you? Bring him to Me." (Mark 9:19)**

It was the disciple's faith that fell short, not God's mercy! Understanding the true root of sickness and pain (explained in chapter 7) makes it clear why Jesus always wants to heal and deliver us. He always wants us to be completely free from the power of Satan and his army! What awesome assurance we should have in God's faithfulness to deliver us from evil!

Let Jesus bless you today. Open your heart and see that He wants you, His precious child, to be strong and healthy in mind, body, and spirit.

> **"I am willing; be cleansed." (Matthew 8:3)**

TESTIMONY: Gary Tragus
Birth Date: July 27, 1970
Occupation: Student
Experience: **Healed of a skin disorder**
Date of Testimony: April 1, 1995

Sometime in the spring of 1993, I was suffering from a skin disorder. I had discoloration on my neck and chest. Spots of discoloration, a loss of pigment to be precise. I was healed by Jesus Christ a few weeks after my symptoms were prevalent. I was healed in our Tae Kwon Do School. It's as black and white as now you have it, now you don't. A few days after my meeting with Master D. J. Kim, the spots disappeared. Pigment began to return to my skin, and I haven't had the infirmity return as to present.

Chapter IX
God's Blessings Are Received by Faith

People from all walks of life have examined God's blessings under a microscope to find out why some are healed and others aren't. Ultimately, the answer lies in faith. Faith is not merely a mental thought process or a feel-good emotion. It is the attitude of our heart.

It is by faith that the people of God throughout history have obtained the promises or "covenants" of God. By faith Abraham became the father of many nations (Genesis 15:5–6), Joshua and Caleb entered the promised land (Numbers 13, 14), Sarah bore a child in her old age (Hebrews 11:11), and by faith that we have access to God's promise of salvation and peace with God (John 3:18; Romans 5:1–2). In the same way, it is by faith we receive the covenanted promise of healing through Jesus Christ (Isaiah 53:4–5). It is impossible to please God without faith.

> **But without faith it is impossible to please Him, for he who comes to God must believe that He is, and that He is a rewarder of those who diligently seek Him. (Hebrews 11:6)**

Ask yourself these simple questions: Do I trust what Jesus Christ says? Do I believe He will do what He promises? If I do believe, how much? The Bible is very clear on this subject, and gives a true reflection of our own heart's attitude toward God. Let's look at the following verses to examine how people's faith determined their blessing.

Now when Jesus had entered Capernaum, a centurion came to Him, pleading with Him, saying, "Lord, my servant is lying at home paralyzed, dreadfully tormented." And Jesus said to him, "I will come and heal him." The centurion answered and said, "Lord, I am not worthy that You should come under my roof. But only speak a word, and my servant will be healed. For I also am a man under authority, having soldiers under me. And I say to this one, 'Go,' and he goes; and to another, 'Come,' and he comes; and to my servant, 'Do this,' and he does it." When Jesus heard it, He marveled, and said to those who followed, "Assuredly, I say to you, I have not found such great faith, not even in Israel! And I say to you that many will come from east and west, and sit down with Abraham, Isaac, and Jacob in the kingdom of heaven. But the sons of the kingdom will be cast out into outer darkness. There will be weeping and gnashing of teeth." Then Jesus said to the centurion, "Go your way; and as you have believed, so let it be done for you." And his servant was healed that same hour. (Matthew 8:5–13)

What brought this man's blessing? It was his faith that Jesus had the power and authority to make his servant well. Jesus explicitly revealed this to him when He said, *"Go your way; and as you have believed, so let it be done for you."* He believed in the word of Jesus Christ so much that he knew Jesus only had to say the word to heal his servant. We need to have this same kind of faith. God's word made and framed the entire world, and there is inherent power in His word. Let's look at another example.

And they lifted up their voices and said, "Jesus, Master, have mercy on us!" So when He saw them, He said to them, "Go, show yourselves to the priests." And so it was that as they went, they were cleansed. And one of them, when he saw that he was healed, returned, and with a loud voice glorified God, and fell down on his face at His feet, giving Him thanks. And he was a Samaritan. So Jesus answered and said, "Were there not ten cleansed? But where are the nine? Were there not any found who returned to give glory to God except this foreigner?" And He said to him, "Arise, go your way. Your faith has made you well." (Luke 17:13–19)

Again, what made the men well? Was it random selection? No! Not at all! Jesus said, *"Your faith has made you well."* Can you imagine it? These people were not even healed immediately! They were healed *"as they went."* They took Jesus at His word! All the potential and provision for healing is within Jesus Christ, but it is faith in Him, and in His promise, that causes His power to flow!

> Then it happened, as He was coming near Jericho, that a certain blind man sat by the road begging. And hearing a multitude passing by, he asked what it meant. So they told him that Jesus of Nazareth was passing by. And he cried out, saying, "Jesus, Son of David, have mercy on me!" Then those who went before warned him that he should be quiet; but he cried out all the more, "Son of David, have mercy on me!" So Jesus stood still and commanded him to be brought to Him. And when he had come near, He asked him, saying, "What do you want Me to do for you?" He said, "Lord, that I may receive my sight." Then Jesus said to him, "Receive your sight; your faith has made you well." And immediately he received his sight, and followed Him, glorifying God. And all the people, when they saw it, gave praise to God. (Luke 18:35–43)

Did you see it? Jesus said, *"Receive your sight; your faith has made you well."* His faith is what made him well.

> And behold, a woman of Canaan came from that region and cried out to Him, saying, "Have mercy on me, O Lord, Son of David! My daughter is severely demon-possessed." But He answered her not a word. And His disciples came and urged Him, saying, "Send her away, for she cries out after us." But He answered and said, "I was not sent except to the lost sheep of the house of Israel." Then she came and worshiped Him, saying, "Lord, help me!" But He answered and said, "It is not good to take the children's bread and throw it to the little dogs." And she said, "Yes, Lord, yet even the little dogs eat the crumbs, which fall from their masters' table. Then Jesus answered and said to her, "O woman, great is your faith! Let it be to you as you desire." And her daughter was healed from that very hour. (Matthew 15:22–28)

Wow! Here is an example of a time where Jesus expressed that He wasn't sent to teach and help the people of Canaan, but was sent to the people of Israel. Despite this, the woman wouldn't give up, and because of her great faith Jesus granted her request!

> When Jesus departed from there, two blind men followed Him, crying out and saying, "Son of David, have mercy on us!" And when He had come into the house, the blind men came to Him. And Jesus said to them, "Do you believe that I am able to do this?" They said to Him, "Yes, Lord." Then He touched their eyes, saying, "According to your faith let it be to you."' And their eyes were opened. And Jesus sternly warned them, saying, See that no one knows it." (Matthew 9:27–30)

In this example, Jesus asked the men, *"Do you believe that I am able to do this?"* Jesus asks the same question of us today. If we respond with a confident "Yes" as they did, we are sure to be touched by Him. It doesn't get any clearer than verse 29: *"According to your faith let it be to you."*

The amount of blessing we receive depends on our faith! A little faith yields a little blessing, while much faith yields much blessing. Praise God that He has not put a limit on the magnitude of blessing we can receive.

> Then they came to Him, bringing a paralytic who was carried by four men. And when they could not come near Him because of the crowd, they uncovered the roof where He was. So when they had broken through, they let down the bed on which the paralytic was lying. When Jesus saw their faith, He said to the paralytic, "Son, your sins are forgiven you." And some of the scribes were sitting there and reasoning in their hearts, "Why does this Man speak blasphemies like this? Who can forgive sins but God alone?" But immediately, when Jesus perceived in His spirit that they reasoned thus within themselves, He said to them, "Why do you reason about these things in your hearts? Which is easier, to say to the paralytic, 'Your sins are forgiven you,' or to say, 'Arise, take up your bed and walk'? But that you may know that the Son of Man has power on

earth to forgive sins"—He said to the paralytic, "I say to
you, arise, take up your bed, and go to your house." Immediately he arose, took up the bed, and went out in the presence of them all, so that all were amazed and glorified God,
saying, "We never saw anything like this!" (Mark 2:3–12)

Here we see that faith prompts believers to take action. It is *not*
enough to sit back and "let go and let God." God requires us to take
action and use our will with perseverance. He meets us more than
halfway, but we need to persevere in faith. If we truly believe, we
will run to Jesus with open arms, and He will heal us. Put 100 percent of your trust in Him rather than the world's wisdom. We can
sometimes fool one another with eloquent speech and say all the
right things, but Jesus knows us better than we know ourselves.
Our actions show whether we believe, and it is by true faith that we
obtain the blessings of God. We will soon read exactly how to take
action to overcome your problems because idle information won't
help unless we act on God's instruction.

And behold, one of the rulers of the synagogue came, Jairus
by name. And when he saw Him, he fell at His feet and
begged Him earnestly, saying, "My little daughter lies at
the point of death. Come and lay Your hands on her, that
she may be healed, and she will live." So Jesus went with
him, and a great multitude followed Him and thronged
Him. Now a certain woman had a flow of blood for twelve
years, and had suffered many things from many physicians.
She had spent all that she had and was no better, but rather
grew worse. When she heard about Jesus, she came behind
Him in the crowd and touched His garment. For she said,
"If only I may touch His clothes, I shall be made well."
Immediately the fountain of her blood was dried up, and
she felt in her body that she was healed of the affliction.
And Jesus, immediately knowing in Himself that power
had gone out of Him, turned around in the crowd and said,
"Who touched My clothes?" But His disciples said to Him,
"You see the multitude thronging You, and You say, 'Who
touched Me?'" And He looked around to see her who had
done this thing. But the woman, fearing and trembling,
knowing what had happened to her, came and fell down
before Him and told Him the whole truth. And He said to

her, "Daughter, your faith has made you well. Go in peace, and be healed of your affliction." (Mark: 5:22–34)

This account is as relevant today as it was then. Why was only this woman healed even though there were many people touching Jesus? Similarly, why are only a few people healed out of thousands who pray? The answer is found in verse 34. Jesus said to her, *"Daughter, your faith has made you well. Go in peace, and be healed of your affliction."* Yes, it was her faith that made her different! Her faith is what caused power to come forth from Jesus Christ. She alone touched Him with intimacy and deep faith. The others only touched Him superficially. Faith is the key to access God's power. Though thousands may pray, only those who truly believe will cause power to come forth from Jesus. This truth is consistently demonstrated in daily life and is testified by millions of people. We need to desire to touch Jesus intimately, and never give up until we truly connect. Look at this example.

> **Now they came to Jericho. As He went out of Jericho with His disciples and a great multitude, blind Bartimaeus, the son of Timaeus, sat by the road begging. And when he heard that it was Jesus of Nazareth, he began to cry out and say, "Jesus, Son of David, have mercy on me!" Then many warned him to be quiet; but he cried out all the more, "Son of David, have mercy on me!" So Jesus stood still and commanded him to be called. Then they called the blind man, saying to him, "Be of good cheer. Rise, He is calling you." And throwing aside his garment, he rose and came to Jesus. So Jesus answered and said to him, "What do you want Me to do for you?" The blind man said to Him, "Rabboni, that I may receive my sight." Then Jesus said to him, "Go your way; your faith has made you well." And immediately he received his sight and followed Jesus on the road. (Mark 10:46–52)**

Do not let anyone distract you from your goal. If this man listened to those around him, he never would have been healed. Pursue Christ with all your heart, and let nothing hinder you. You must persevere in faith no matter what distractions or difficulties may try to hinder you.

So Jesus came again to Cana of Galilee where He had made the water wine. And there was a certain nobleman whose son was sick at Capernaum. When he heard that Jesus had come out of Judea into Galilee, he went to Him and implored Him to come down and heal his son, for he was at the point of death. Then Jesus said to him, "Unless you people see signs and wonders, you will by no means believe." The nobleman said to Him, "Sir, come down before my child dies!" Jesus said to him, "Go your way; your son lives." So the man believed the word that Jesus spoke to him, and he went his way. And as he was now going down, his servants met him and told him, saying, "Your son lives!" Then he inquired of them the hour when he got better. And they said to him, "Yesterday at the seventh hour the fever left him." So the father knew that it was at the same hour in which Jesus said to him, "Your son lives." And he himself believed, and his whole household. (John 4:46–53)

This is another example where this man believed Jesus without receiving any other sign or indication that anything had changed. There was no proof at all when Jesus told him, *"Go your way; your son lives."* It was by faith the man returned home believing that he already received what Jesus promised him.

For whatever is born of God overcomes the world. And this is the victory that has overcome the world—our faith. Who is he who overcomes the world, but he who believes that Jesus is the Son of God? (1 John 5:4–5)

This truth must be paramount in your mind and life. This is direct instruction on how to overcome the world. Believe that Jesus Christ is the Son of God, and your faith will make you more than conqueror over every trial and tribulation. Even if we are unaware of the cause of our problems, but fully believe in His promise, we receive His blessing! What awesome assurance!

Now this is the confidence that we have in Him, that if we ask anything according to His will, He hears us. And if we know that He hears us, whatever we ask, we know that we have the petitions that we have asked of Him. (1 John 5:14–15)

"And whatever things you ask in prayer, believing, you will
receive." (Matthew 21:22)

We have learned it is God's will for you to be healed and to
overcome every one of your struggles. We know that if we ask
anything according to His will, God hears our prayer, and we have
the requests we asked for! This means there must be no room for
doubt. Failure is not an option for a praying Christian in the will of
God. Have an attitude that focuses only on the promises of God,
and refuse to look to the left or the right. Remember that God works
faithfully through His covenants and *will* keep His word.

TESTIMONY: Loretta Deragio
Birth Date: June 25, 1947
Occupation: Customer Service
Experience: **Healed of a lump on her neck**
Date of Testimony: August 3, 1999

Master Kim knew something was troubling me. I didn't look
happy, I didn't smile, and I looked sick. Master Kim started teaching me about the Bible, and many things that I didn't know. I
was worrying that I had cancer. I had a lump on my neck, and
couldn't carry anything in my right hand because it would hurt
my neck. Master Kim told me about the demons that overcome
us, and how this did not have to be the case. We prayed and
Master Kim cast the demons from me in the name of Jesus
Christ. I felt a hot sensation in the right side of my chest, and it
flew out of me. This happened three times that evening. I felt
something leave my body, and the experience was unique. I
felt like 50 pounds was lifted from my chest. It was easier to
breathe, and I was completely relaxed. I've been smiling ever
since. Since learning about the Bible, and the casting out of
demons, I have been a more understanding person, and the
lump on my neck is gone! I can now carry bags and packages
in my right hand, and it doesn't hurt anymore. When difficult
times arise in my life, I just handle it differently now. Before I
get angry, I stop and make a decision to not let the demons
back in. I'm truly thankful to God, and am most grateful to Master Kim for his servant's heart for Jesus.

Chapter X
Why Some Don't Overcome

Prayer to overcome difficulty is one of the most common requests made to God, and still challenges many Christians. We sit in awe trying to reconcile the difference between the greatness of God's promises and the lack of victory in our lives. We so often feel discouraged wondering why God hasn't done His job. If God promised that Jesus Christ would take away all of our sickness and disease, then why do we still have them? Why didn't our prayer work? Why are only a few healed among innumerable masses? Why do we still live as if we were still under the curse? This quandary often leads to great confusion, discouragement, and, in some cases, even anger. These are good critical questions, which so rarely receive honest answers.

The following look at God's word reveals that we've got it all wrong. God has indeed completed His work through Jesus Christ and has already prepared every blessing for us with no desire of holding it back. The fact is that we ourselves are the cause for lack of victory...not God. This is incredibly great news since we can avoid our mistakes and finally enjoy victory! Let's examine some of the pitfalls which hinder us from living in God's "promised land" of blessing.

Unbelief

As discussed in chapter 9, the way to receive God's promised blessings is by faith. Conversely, the paramount reason for *not* receiving God's promised blessings is simply a lack of faith. When we pray for healing, do we truly anticipate a full recovery? Do we exhibit the excitement and jubilee of being delivered from our trouble, or do we continue to hang our heads as if our prayer didn't change anything? The sad reality is that many only have a faint hope they will recover. In fact, expectations are sometimes so low that prayer feels more like a burdensome obligation rather than a tremendous life-giving opportunity! We so quickly profess to believe, but with honest introspection we realize there is doubt lingering in our hearts like a dark cloud preventing the sun from shining brightly. The Bible calls us to a faith which is not partial, but complete, and wholly given to trust in God's word. This means there can be *no* doubt. Look at what Jesus Christ said.

> So Jesus answered and said to them, "Assuredly, I say to you, if you have faith and do not doubt, you will not only do what was done to the fig tree, but also if you say to this mountain, 'Be removed and be cast into the sea,' it will be done. And whatever things you ask in prayer, believing, you will receive." (Matthew 21:21–22)

Though people may complicate the issues of prayer and faith, Jesus gave straightforward answers. He plainly said that *"if"* we have faith and *"do not doubt,"*...it will be done! There should be no confusion. If we pray, and are not *"believing,"* we will not receive! Let's take another look at this same point.

> But let him ask in faith, with no doubting, for he who doubts is like a wave of the sea driven and tossed by the wind. For let not that man suppose that he will receive anything from the Lord; he is a double-minded man, unstable in all his ways. (James 1:6)

God is communicating a powerful message through this verse. It addresses that sometimes we have a double mind. Part of our mind believes in the fulfillment of God's promise, while another part of our mind doubts the same promise. This is where we think we may be healed, but are not completely sure. We are part believing and part unbelieving. God tells us this condition causes instability in all of our ways, and that we should not even expect, anticipate, or look to receive the blessing in any way, shape or form. It is critical to overcome a double mind so that we can stand strong in God's promises.

Let's see this faith principle in action when Jesus was physically on earth. What happened when Jesus came face to face with unbelief?

> When He had come to His own country, He taught them in their synagogue, so that they were astonished and said, "Where did this Man get this wisdom and these mighty works? Is this not the carpenter's son? Is not His mother called Mary? And His brothers James, Joses, Simon, and Judas? And His sisters, are they not all with us? Where then did this Man get all these things?" So they were offended at Him. But Jesus said to them, "A prophet is not without honor except in his own country and in his own house." Now He did not do many mighty works there because of their unbelief. (Matthew 13:54–58)

> Now He could do no mighty work there, except that He laid His hands on a few sick people and healed them. And He marveled because of their unbelief. Then He went about the villages in a circuit, teaching. (Mark 6:5–7)

Is this not the same result we witness today? Many pray, but few are healed. In this example, Jesus laid hands on only a few sick people, but was unable to do mighty work because of their unbelief. It wasn't that Jesus was unwilling, He was hindered by their unbelief. As stated, God will not and cannot deny Himself. God requires faith to bless, and faith was not found in these people. Faith is placed inside each believer as a seed that must grow. Faith is not a feeling, but rather a much deeper assurance that God keeps His word.

> Now faith is the substance of things hoped for, the evidence of things not seen. (Hebrews 11:1)

Where we place our focus is where we end up. When we focus our thoughts and actions on the word of God, that is exactly where we will be living. If our thoughts and actions are focused on pains, problems, and difficulties, that is where we will dwell. We can see this principle in action when Peter, one of Jesus' followers, got out of a boat, walked on water, and then...

> **Now in the fourth watch of the night Jesus went to them, walking on the sea. And when the disciples saw Him walking on the sea, they were troubled, saying, "It is a ghost!" And they cried out for fear. But immediately Jesus spoke to them, saying, "Be of good cheer! It is I; do not be afraid." And Peter answered Him and said, "Lord, if it is You, command me to come to You on the water." So He said, "Come." And when Peter had come down out of the boat, he walked on the water to go to Jesus. But when he saw that the wind was boisterous, he was afraid; and beginning to sink he cried out, saying, "Lord, save me!" And immediately Jesus stretched out His hand and caught him, and said to him, "O you of little faith, why did you doubt?" And when they got into the boat, the wind ceased. Then those who were in the boat came and worshiped Him, saying, "Truly You are the Son of God." (Matthew 14:25–33)**

Peter had faith! He got out of the boat! This faith is what enabled him to accomplish what seemed impossible. He focused on Jesus, and it enabled him to rise above every natural law that would have previously held him back. Then something changed. Peter took his focus off Jesus, and put it onto the trouble around him. He saw the power of the wind and became afraid. It was at this point that he began to sink. His lack of faith at that moment immediately impacted his ability to follow Jesus' words, which said, *"Come."* This principle holds true for you and I when we take our focus off Jesus. We begin to sink into the very trouble we are trying to break free from. The answer then is to stay focused on Jesus and believe with no doubting!

"...Do not be unbelieving, but believing." (John 20:27)

Our faith, like our muscles, is either in a state of growth or decline. There is never status quo. We must, therefore, be diligent to continually grow our faith through reading the Bible, meditating on God's word, and obeying His commands.

> **So then faith comes by hearing, and hearing by the word of God. (Romans 10:17)**

When we fail to read the Bible and obey God, our faith becomes weakened and sometimes ineffective. This is why it is so crucial to train with great effort so that your faith will be strong and unshakable. Cast your doubt aside, and make the decision to believe in God's promises 100 percent. Realize that prayer is direct and personal communication with God. Never lose sight that God not only hears but feels the cry of His children, and is ready to respond with great power!

Sin

Sin stops us dead in our tracks in every area of spiritual growth. Sin poisons our lives, and has the power to bind with every kind of burden and trouble.

> **Blessed is the man who endures temptation; for when he has been approved, he will receive the crown of life, which the Lord has promised to those who love Him. Let no one say when he is tempted, "I am tempted by God;" for God cannot be tempted by evil, nor does He Himself tempt anyone. But each one is tempted when he is drawn away by his own desires and enticed. Then, when desire has conceived, it gives birth to sin; and sin, when it is full-grown, brings forth death. (James 1:12–15)**

We must immediately confess and turn away (repent) from our sin so that Jesus can forgive us when we fall. When we choose to follow our desire for sin over the will of God, we are essentially choosing to do the will of Satan over the will of God. When we are being led by sin, we are being led by the devil, and are not standing strong in the freedom Jesus Christ has provided.

> **Do you not know that to whom you present yourselves slaves to obey, you are that one's slaves whom you obey,**

> whether of sin leading to death, or of obedience leading to righteousness? (Romans 6:16)

Recognize sin in your life and strike it out! So many believe living with sin is unavoidable and just part of being human. They say, "It's human nature, and we can't avoid it." To a certain degree, they're correct. Human nature is sinful, and the flesh does not desire the things of the spirit. This is why Jesus Christ gave us a new nature with a spiritual body that desires to live according to the will of God. The flesh and the spirit will always war against one another, but we must make a conscious choice to overcome sin and obey Jesus Christ.

> This I say, therefore, and testify in the Lord, that you should no longer walk as the rest of the Gentiles walk, in the futility of their mind, having their understanding darkened, being alienated from the life of God, because of the ignorance that is in them, because of the blindness of their heart; who, being past feeling, have given themselves over to lewdness, to work all uncleanness with greediness. But you have not so learned Christ, if indeed you have heard Him and have been taught by Him, as the truth is in Jesus: that you put off, concerning your former conduct, the old man which grows corrupt according to the deceitful lusts, and be renewed in the spirit of your mind, and that you put on the new man which was created according to God, in true righteousness and holiness. (Ephesians 4:17–24)

All sin blocks God's power and reduces the effectiveness of our prayer. We must do our best to abide in Jesus Christ so that we can bear the fruits of righteousness and live in His blessings.

> "Abide in Me, and I in you. As the branch cannot bear fruit of itself, unless it abides in the vine, neither can you, unless you abide in Me. I am the vine, you are the branches. He who abides in Me, and I in him, bears much fruit; for without Me you can do nothing." (John 15:4–5)

Remember that sin is "missing the mark" that God has intended for us, and includes more than just immorality. It includes every command of God no matter how trivial they may appear.

But he who doubts is condemned if he eats, because he does not eat from faith; for whatever is not from faith is sin. (Romans 14:23)

Even doubt is sin, *"for whatever is not from faith is sin."* This is partly why doubting the promises of God hinders us from receiving God's blessings. Imagine a lifeline connected between you and God. When connected, God's power is able to flow through you. Now imagine a broken line so no power could reach you leaving you with only your strength. This is exactly what happens when we are in a state of sin, fear, and doubt. The line of God's power flowing to us becomes obstructed.

Another devastating sin is pride. When pride exists in our hearts and minds, it means we think we are stronger than we really are. It means we wrongfully exalt ourselves above our proper place and position, and makes it difficult to fully submit to Jesus. Pride is one of the subtlest traps Satan uses to bind the children of God. It can prevent God's promises from becoming reality because it produces an attitude that we know better than God. We must always keep our hearts and minds bowed before the majesty and greatness of God.

Pride goes before destruction, And a haughty spirit before a fall. (Proverbs 16:18)

The Bible even says:

Likewise you younger people, submit yourselves to your elders. Yes, all of you be submissive to one another, and be clothed with humility, for "God resists the proud, But gives grace to the humble." Therefore humble yourselves under the mighty hand of God, that He may exalt you in due time, casting all your care upon Him, for He cares for you. (1 Peter 5:5–7)

Jesus is very clear when He says we need to approach God with a humble and contrite spirit to be blessed.

"For the hearts of this people have grown dull. Their ears are hard of hearing, And their eyes they have closed, Lest

they should see with their eyes and hear with their ears,
Lest they should understand with their hearts and turn,
So that I should heal them." (Matthew 13:15)

Hard and prideful hearts prevent blessing. Open your heart and come to Him in humble supplication to ensure God's grace will abound in your life.

Our weaknesses should not be cause for frustration and discouragement. They only mean that we need to strive toward greater faith and victory over sin. Spiritual growth takes time. It has been said that it takes a moment to trust Jesus as our Savior, but a lifetime to walk blamelessly. Nevertheless, know that God faithfully gives us power to overcome every sin and weakness in our lives.

No temptation has overtaken you except such as is common to man; but God is faithful, who will not allow you to be tempted beyond what you are able, but with the temptation will also make the way of escape, that you may be able to bear it. (1 Corinthians 10:13)

"If you do well, will you not be accepted? And if you do not do well, sin lies at the door. And its desire is for you, but you should rule over it." (Genesis 4:7)

God's Armor Forgotten

When we successfully pray, and overcome the power of the enemy within, the struggle is far from over. Satan and his army never roll over in defeat. They are in a never-ending pursuit to kill, steal, and destroy. (John 10:10) Every time we let down our guard, and fall into sin, we give them opportunity to gain a foothold in our lives. This is why we must protect our minds and bodies allowing nothing but the glory and power of God to reign in us.

"When an unclean spirit goes out of a man, he goes through dry places, seeking rest, and it finds none. Then he says, 'I will return to my house from which I came.' And when he comes, he finds it empty, swept and put in order. Then he goes and takes with him seven other spirits more wicked than himself, and they enter and dwell there; and the last

state of that man is worse than the first. So shall it also be with this wicked generation." (Matthew 12:43–45)

This passage describes our bodies as a house. After an unclean spirit leaves, it goes through *"dry places"* looking to enter another body. Then, after finding none, returns back to its original house with re-inforcements. Upon entering, they find the house *"put in order"* or healthy. Now more spirits enter the person resulting in an even greater struggle. This is exactly why Jesus warned a man who was healed to *"sin no more!"* It's very dangerous to give the devil an opportunity by falling into sin.

Afterward Jesus found him in the temple, and said to him, "See, you have been made well. Sin no more, lest a worse thing come upon you." (John 5:14)

Strive to walk in the spirit, and not according to the flesh. The less we fall into sin, the less opportunity the devil will have to harm us.

"I Can Do It On My Own"

Another reason we struggle with defeat is that we rely on our own strength. When we rely on our strength alone, we are defeated before we even begin. Relying on the power of Jesus Christ ensures success. In the Garden of Eden, Adam and Eve stopped relying on God and relied on their own abilities. We should be careful not to fall into the same trap. There is only One who can save and deliver from the devil's attacks—the Lord Jesus Christ. This is why the Bible says,

Finally, my brethren, be strong in the Lord and in the power of His might. (Ephesians 6:10)

Standing strong in the power and might of the Lord means relying wholly on His power. We are to put on the full armor of God, show up for battle, raise the sword of the spirit which is the word of God, and then let God's power do the rest. Standing strong is a combined effort of our action and God's power. Just hoping that God is going to help does not bring victory. Faith and action are inseparable. We should not expect success in conquering trials and tribulations unless we heed God's call to action! Here is a description of the action necessary to win the struggle with evil.

> **Therefore submit to God. Resist the devil and he will flee from you. (James 4:7)**

We must submit and resist. First, we must let go of our strength and wisdom and submit our will to God. Then, we must resist the devil. Notice we are not called to resist a situation or particular problem. We are called to resist the "one" behind them, the devil. Upon doing these things, God's power takes action, and causes the devil to flee from us. Don't let the devil trick you to think it is all your power or all God's responsibility. Gideon, one of the greatest Judges of Israel, understood this concept when he charged into battle. He knew he had to show up and fight the enemy, but knew it was God who would produce his victory. It's a combined effort.

> **"When I blow the trumpet, I and all who are with me, then you also blow the trumpets on every side of the whole camp, and say, 'The sword of the LORD and of Gideon!'" (Judges 7:18)**

Faith produces the kind of action that requires the help of God. Attempting to stand strong without God working with us to produce victory is nothing short of futile. We should be doers of His word with faith that God will be working with us. This is why faith and works must go together.

> **Therefore lay aside all filthiness and overflow of wickedness, and receive with meekness the implanted word, which is able to save your souls. But be doers of the word, and not hearers only, deceiving yourselves. For if anyone is a hearer of the word and not a doer, he is like a man observing his natural face in a mirror; for he observes himself, goes away, and immediately forgets what kind of man he was. But he who looks into the perfect law of liberty and continues in it, and is not a forgetful hearer but a doer of the work, this one will be blessed in what he does. (James 1:21–25)**

Thus also faith by itself, if it does not have works, is dead. (James 2:17)

We Forget the Root

Another common reason people do not overcome their problems is that they do not take specific action against the cause. We are commanded to hit the enemy straight on and deal with the real root of the problem exactly as Jesus Christ did. There is no difference between the root of your sickness and those we have read in the Bible. All sickness, problems, and disease, whether physical, mental, or spiritual, ultimately have their root in the spiritual realm. All other methods outside the teaching in the Bible do nothing but leave us cheated of God's best. Overcome the enemy, and you will overcome your problems no matter what they may be.

> **Beware lest anyone cheat you through philosophy and empty deceit, according to the tradition of men, according to the basic principles of the world, and not according to Christ. For in Him dwells all the fullness of the Godhead bodily; and you are complete in Him, who is the head of all principality and power. (Colossians 2:8–10)**

Soon, we will cover how to remove the enemy exactly as Jesus did.

TESTIMONY: Cezar Muzones
Birth Date: December 12, 1968
Occupation: Senior Programmer Analyst
Experience: **Healed from salmonella poisoning effects (acute enteritis), four pinched nerves, a knee injury, and the flu**
Date of Testimony: February 18, 1999

I have suffered from several ailments and a slew of miscellaneous injuries. I had four pinched nerves on my back, both knees were in bad shape from years of tackle football, I was struck by a car three to four times as a child, and nearly lost my right eye in a sports accident. One ailment that had lasting repercussions until this date was my acute enteritis. I contracted a salmonella infection from some semi-raw eggs I had eaten. I lost almost 20 pounds within a week's time, and I was hospitalized the following week. My digestive system was affected by the experience, and I found myself easily nauseated from any odd taste, sick joke, or graphical image. Even the very memory of my illness caused me to be nauseated. I wasn't able to try any new foods for fear of getting sick. I finally spoke to Master Kim about my recurring back injury that I was experiencing at the time. He asked me if I was a religious man. I answered, "Yes". I thought very highly of Master Kim, and saw no harm in hearing him out. We went on to discuss the domains of heaven and hell, the influence of the devil, and his minions. He showed me the testimonies of others God helped before me, and I was surprised by some of them. Only by believing and accepting Jesus as our Savior can we fight off the influences of the devil and be saved. Master Kim prayed for me, laid his hands on my head to cast the demon out of my body, and I fell to the ground. I remember going into the room before prayer and found the room cold and extremely chilly. After prayer I found myself warm and comfortable. It's hard to describe how I felt immediately afterward, but I was disoriented and overwhelmed. The back pain I originally started with was gone, the cold/flu that I was suffering subsided to an occasional sniffle, and my taunting knee pain was reduced to nothing. I have since tested my feeling of nausea, and found that I can sample new foods without getting ill!

Chapter XI
Common Misperceptions

Misperception #1: Sometimes it is God's will for us to be sick.

The belief that it is God's will for us to be sick is another great deception of the devil. It may appear noble to some to endure sickness and pain for the glory of God, but this is contrary to God's will. The Bible teaches that we are going to experience difficulty and tribulation, but that we should overcome these things in the power and grace of Jesus Christ.

> **Who shall separate us from the love of Christ? Shall tribulation, or distress, or persecution, or famine, or nakedness, or peril, or sword? As it is written: "For Your sake we are killed all day long; We are accounted as sheep for the slaughter." Yet in all these things we are more than conquerors through Him who loved us. For I am persuaded that neither death nor life, nor angels nor principalities nor powers, nor things present nor things to come, nor height nor depth, nor any other created thing, shall be able to separate us from the love of God which is in Christ Jesus our Lord. (Romans 8:35–39)**

Trials and tribulations should spur spiritual growth and development in our lives. They should help produce our sanctification (setting apart), and never our destruction.

> My brethren, count it all joy when you fall into various
> trials, knowing that the testing of your faith produces pa-
> tience. But let patience have its perfect work, that you may
> be perfect and complete, lacking nothing. (James 1:2–4)

The Old Testament prophecy concerning Jesus Christ says, *"And
by His stripes we are healed"* (Isaiah 53:5). It does not say, "We are healed
in some cases" or "healed except when..." The Bible makes it clear
that Jesus poured out His power, love, and blessing to *all* those who
believe. We see Jesus' desire to share His promise with everyone.

> When the sun was setting, all those who had any that were
> sick with various diseases brought them to Him; and He
> laid His hands on every one of them and healed them. And
> demons also came out of many, crying out and saying, "You
> are the Christ, the Son of God!" And He, rebuking them,
> did not allow them to speak, for they knew that He was the
> Christ. (Luke 4:40–41)

To fully understand this truth, let's look deeper into who we
are in God's eyes as believers in Jesus Christ. The Bible says that
God's children are actually temples of His Spirit!

> Do you not know that you are the temple of God and that
> the Spirit of God dwells in you? (1 Corinthians 3:16)

God's spirit does not dwell in the buildings we call churches.
God's spirit dwells within us. We have become temples of His Holy
Spirit! God's presence is in church because we are in church and the
Holy Spirit is in us!

> Or do you not know that your body is the temple of the
> Holy Spirit who is in you, whom you have from God, and
> you are not your own? For you were bought at a price; there-
> fore glorify God in your body and in your spirit, which are
> God's. (1 Corinthians 6:19–20)

Yes! Our bodies belong to God and have been purchased
with the blood of Jesus Christ! We are all members of the body of
Christ! When Jesus Christ heals, and takes care of us, He is taking care of His property, and part of the collective body of Christ!
Our perspective on healing changes completely when we realize

God is intimately and intensely involved in our welfare, and wants us to be healthy in mind, body, and spirit. We are His children and part of His body!

We should have absolute assurance God will heal because deliverance has been covenanted to everyone who believes. God is not in heaven making new decisions about who to heal, and when. He has already made the decision that *all* who believe will be blessed, and wants us to receive His blessings *all* the time. We shouldn't be waiting for sporadic spurts of power to fall from heaven. We should unceasingly abide in His blessings and power. Do not be tricked into believing that it isn't God's time to heal you. God's time to deliver His promise was over 2,000 years ago when He sent His Son to die for our sins. Jesus Christ already came, already died, already rose from the dead, and already defeated the enemy! If you believe in Jesus, don't wait for the promise any longer, live in the promise. Look closely at the verb *tense* of this promise:

...Who Himself bore our sins in His own body on the tree, that we, having died to sins, might live for righteousness— by whose stripes you were healed. (1 Peter 2:24)

When Jesus died on the cross, and rose on the third day, the devil's power was completely destroyed. Most just never have the opportunity to find out! Don't be tricked into thinking that God wants you to needlessly suffer with pain. God wants us to take the difficulty in our lives and transform it into a time of training and development. There is no mistake that life can be extremely tough, and anyone who disagrees isn't living in it. We must strive with great determination to stand. There is invaluable growth which takes place in the life of a believer when we work through our troubles in a godly manner.

My brethren, count it all joy when you fall into various trials, knowing that the testing of your faith produces patience. But let patience have its perfect work, that you may be perfect and complete, lacking nothing. (James 1:2–4)

Hardship forces us to apply the word of God, and develops a deep level of trust in our Father. When you endure and persevere with faith, the only possible outcome is VICTORY! It may not happen overnight, but it will happen. Even Job, a great man of God, went through intense tribulation, submitted to the sovereignty of God, and emerged with far greater blessings than before. (Job 42:12)

There is possibly no greater faith builder than trusting God's word in the face of distress and winning! It is by this very experience that we bring great glory to Jesus Christ. Christianity is much more a demonstration of God's power than a discourse in theology.

> **And my speech and my preaching were not with persuasive words of human wisdom, but in demonstration of the Spirit and of power, that your faith should not be in the wisdom of men but in the power of God. (1 Corinthians 2:4–5)**

Though difficult times will come, we must always give awesome thanks to God for His grace, mercy, and provision, knowing that with faith and perseverance, we <u>will</u> be made victorious.

Misperception #2: That Was Then, This is Now.

Some think Biblical times were different than our modern age. They say Jesus cast out demons then, but it doesn't work the same way today. They claim that Jesus works through medicines to heal instead, and it isn't necessary to follow His example of old. This belief is inconsistent with the teachings of the Bible because the root of our problems hasn't changed since Eden, and neither has God's solution.

The spiritual world, which existed before earth's creation, is the same spiritual world existing today. No modern advances in technology can alter it, and this is why we still face the same spiritual issues as people in Biblical times. The spiritual world is just as active today as it was then. Satan wants people to forget about the spiritual world and cling to modern methods, knowing that he gains strength the moment we shift our focus away from Jesus Christ. We must understand that God's will is unchangeable, and that Biblical teachings are timeless.

> **Jesus Christ is the same yesterday, today, and forever. (Hebrews 13:8)**

For I am the Lord, I do not change;... (Malachi 3:6)

If Jesus healed 2,000 years ago, then Jesus heals today! If the power of Jesus Christ cast demons out 2,000 years ago, then His power casts demons out today. Man's knowledge constantly changes, but the ways and promises of God are immutable. God's ways will always be far greater than ours.

> **"For My thoughts are not your thoughts, Nor are your ways My ways," says the Lord. "For as the heavens are higher than the earth, So are My ways higher than your ways, And my thoughts than your thoughts." (Isaiah 55:8–9)**

Do not allow yourself to be cheated of God's knowledge and blessing by adhering to the basic principles of this world.

> **Let no one deceive himself. If anyone among you seems to be wise in this age, let him become a fool that he may become wise. For the wisdom of this world is foolishness with God. For it is written, "He catches the wise in their own craftiness." (1 Corinthians 3:18–19)**

Misperception #3: Evil Minds its Own Business.

Another tool the devil uses to prevent Christians from resisting him is fear. Fear of the devil has prevented people from learning how to stand strong against the daily influence of Satan. He tricks them into thinking it is too dangerous to engage in spiritual warfare. Or he tricks them into believing they shouldn't study the spiritual world because they are getting involved with evil. They hope that if they stay away from evil, evil will somehow stay away from them. Nothing could be further from the truth since the Bible teaches that evil is looking for us and seeking to devour us. Resisting the devil isn't an option, it's a necessity!

> **Be sober, be vigilant; because your adversary the devil walks about like a roaring lion, seeking whom he may devour. Resist him, steadfast in the faith, knowing that the same sufferings are experienced by your brotherhood in the world. (1 Peter 5:8–9)**

Rest assured that resisting the devil has nothing to do with getting involved with evil, and everything to do with getting rid of evil! The casting out of demons is a manifestation of the power of God and should never be feared.

> **Then one was brought to Him who was demon-possessed, blind and mute; and He healed him, so that the blind and mute man both spoke and saw. And all the multitudes were amazed and said, "Could this be the Son of David?" Now when the Pharisees heard it they said, "This fellow does not cast out demons except by Beelzebub, the ruler of the demons." But Jesus knew their thoughts, and said to them: "Every kingdom divided against itself is brought to desolation, and every city or house divided against itself will not stand. If Satan casts out Satan, he is divided against himself. How then will his kingdom stand? And if I cast out demons by Beelzebub, by whom do your sons cast them out? Therefore they shall be your judges. But if I cast out demons by the Spirit of God, surely the kingdom of God has come upon you. Or how can one enter a strong man's house and plunder his goods, unless he first binds the strong man? And then he will plunder his house. He who is not with Me is against Me, and he who does not gather with Me scatters abroad." (Matthew 12:22–30)**

When we follow the example Jesus Christ set, we can rest assured that we are following the will of God. Realize that we are in the middle of spiritual warfare and must stand strong in the Lord's power to resist the enemy. Ignoring this spiritual struggle will never make it go away. Engage in the resistance of evil, and you will undoubtedly experience the glory of God and live a life filled with victory.

> **And He was preaching in their synagogues throughout all Galilee, and casting out demons. (Mark 1:39)**

Misperception #4: It's Impossible.

When confronted with minor problems, most remain calm with the assurance that God is able to help. When more severe problems arise however, we all too often shrink back in fear, doubt, and anxiety. It is in this moment that we must remember the faithfulness and power of Jesus Christ is independent of the severity, timing, or type of problem. Though something may be impossible for man, it is possible with God. Look at your problem from God's perspective and no difficulty will seem great.

> **But Jesus looked at them and said to them, "With men this is impossible, but with God all things are possible." (Matthew 19:26)**

Even when sickness and disease have taken their toll, and it appears all hope is lost, God can still restore. Jesus not only healed those near death but restored those already dead! Never fear the severity of a sickness because it is irrelevant in the face of unshakable faith.

> **Then Jesus, again groaning in Himself, came to the tomb. It was a cave, and a stone lay against it. Jesus said, "Take away the stone." Martha, the sister of him who was dead, said to Him, "Lord, by this time there is a stench, for he has been dead four days." Jesus said to her, "Did I not say to you that if you would believe you would see the glory of God?" Then they took away the stone from the place where the dead man was lying. And Jesus lifted up His eyes and said, "Father, I thank You that You have heard Me. And I know that You always hear Me, but because of the people who are standing by I said this, that they may believe that You sent Me." Now when He had said these things, He cried with a loud voice, "Lazarus, come forth!" And he who had died came out bound hand and foot with grave clothes, and his face was wrapped with a cloth. Jesus said to them, "Loose him, and let him go." (John 11:38–44)**

Lazarus was dead for four days! Logic and reason may have dictated to give up, but the power of God is held back by neither of these things. Jesus only had to say the word and life returned! Nothing is too hard for God, and we should never live as if it is. Let's take a look at a number of other examples:

> **And Moses said, "The people whom I am among are six hundred thousand men on foot; yet You have said, 'I will**

give them meat, that they may eat for a whole month.' Shall flocks and herds be slaughtered for them, to provide enough for them? Or shall all the fish of the sea be gathered together for them, to provide enough for them?" And the LORD said to Moses, "Has the LORD's arm been shortened?" (Numbers 11:21–23)

While He was still speaking, someone came from the ruler of the synagogue's house, saying to him, "Your daughter is dead. Do not trouble the Teacher." But when Jesus heard it, He answered him, saying, "Do not be afraid; only believe, and she will be made well." When He came into the house, He permitted no one to go in except Peter, James, and John, and the father and mother of the girl. Now all wept and mourned for her; but He said, "Do not weep; she is not dead, but sleeping." And they ridiculed Him, knowing that she was dead. But He put them all outside, took her by the hand and called, saying, "Little girl, arise." Then her spirit returned, and she arose immediately. And He commanded that she be given something to eat. And her parents were astonished, but He charged them to tell no one what had happened. (Luke 8:49–56)

Now it happened, the day after, that He went into a city called Nain; and many of His disciples went with Him, and a large crowd. And when He came near the gate of the city, behold, a dead man was being carried out, the only son of his mother; and she was a widow. And a large crowd from the city was with her. When the Lord saw her, He had compassion on her and said to her, "Do not weep." Then He came and touched the open coffin, and those who carried him stood still. And He said, "Young man, I say to you, arise." So he who was dead sat up and began to speak. And He presented him to his mother. Then fear came upon all, and they glorified God, saying, "A great prophet has risen up among us"; and, "God has visited His people." And this report about Him went throughout all Judea and all the surrounding region. (Luke 7:11–17)

To a person with strong faith, the greater the problem, the greater the opportunity to give glory to God. No problem, difficulty, sickness, or weakness is greater than the Lord, and nothing is impossible for those who believe!

Misperception #5: Demons Only Bother the Wicked.

A common misunderstanding is that the devil's army cannot bother Christians the same way they bother nonbelievers. Some hold that because a believer has been made new in the spirit, their flesh is impervious to the same evil influence. This is ironic given that Christians suffer the very same difficulties as non-Christians. If the Bible demonstrates that evil spirits are inside the body causing sickness, pain, and destruction (chapter 7), and Christians suffer from the same sickness, pain, and destruction as everyone else, how can we say that a Christian is exempt from this kind of attack? As stated earlier, the difference between a Christian and a non-Christian is not the way the devil can attack, but rather their position and ability to overcome. Most Christians have an understanding that evil is behind their problems, but are unaware of where the evil is working. This confusion has prevented many Christians from waging successful spiritual warfare. It is no wonder why so many Christians still live oppressed by the devil!

Christians Need Armor

The apostle Paul wrote a letter to the Ephesian church, whose believers were extremely rich in faith. Paul exhorted these believers on a number of topics and finished with one of their greatest needs—spiritual warfare. It was this faithful church that was instructed to put on the full armor of God!

> **Finally, my brethren, be strong in the Lord and in the power of His might. Put on the whole armor of God, that you may be able to stand against the wiles of the devil. For we do not wrestle against flesh and blood, but against principalities, against powers, against the rulers of the darkness of this age, against spiritual hosts of wickedness in the heavenly places. Therefore take up the whole armor of God, that you may be able to withstand in the evil day, and having done all, to stand. Stand therefore, having girded your waist with truth, having put on the breastplate of righteousness, and having shod your feet with the preparation of**

the gospel of peace; above all, taking the shield of faith with which you will be able to quench all the fiery darts of the wicked one. And take the helmet of salvation, and the sword of the Spirit, which is the word of God; praying always with all prayer and supplication in the Spirit, being watchful to this end with all perseverance and supplication for all the saints... (Ephesians 6:10–18)

Paul was telling his audience that "finally" ensure that you do not leave yourself unequipped for spiritual battle. He explained that "we"—talking about himself and his brethren—do not wrestle against flesh and blood, but wrestle against spiritual hosts of wickedness. This is not a battle where arrows are thrown from a distance, but a close wrestling. Yes, we are sanctified and redeemed by the cleansing blood of Jesus Christ, but nevertheless, we are commanded to take up the whole armor of God that we may be able to stand. This literally means that if we as Christians do not put on the full armor of God and effectively wield the sword of the spirit, we will be unable to stand against the wiles of the devil. We will be unable to stand against his methods of killing, stealing, and destroying which include sickness, disease, violence, and many more. This battle is not trivial and is a matter of life and death.

Christians are in no way exempt from any of type of attack from the devil. These exhortations were given to strong Christians. We all must put on the full armor of God and resist the enemy. It is the armor that prevents the *"fiery darts"* from getting in.

Strong believers walking in the strength and power of Jesus Christ are a great threat to Satan's kingdom; consequently, they receive greater attention. It is these people who Satan works especially hard to discourage, beat down, and destroy. It is the believer who understands his/her position in Christ and can overcome. This is why bad things often happen to good people, and the wicked appear to have it easy. The wicked are already lost, and the good are trying to be pulled down! Jesus even prayed for our protection against the devil because of how dangerous he is in the life of a believer.

"I do not pray that You should take them out of the world, but that You should keep them from the evil one." (John 17:15)

Though God has appointed everyone in this life to eventually die, it is never His will for anyone to be murdered by the destroyer. God gave His armor and weapons of spiritual warfare to believers so they could resist and win. We may not be able to escape the fact that we are living in a fallen world where the devil operates, but we can stand strong and steadfast against the enemy in the strength of Jesus Christ. We are no longer slaves to the enemy's power! Resist these forces of darkness with infallible faith and courage, and you will have victory over every trial and tribulation. This is God's promise.

Therefore submit to God. Resist the devil and he will flee from you. (James 4:7)

Spirit and Flesh: They Aren't the Same.

Many contend that evil spirits cannot enter the body that has been made new in Christ. They are 100 percent correct because they can't. They can, however, enter the body that has not been made new in Christ. This may appear like a contradiction until we realize that both bodies exist in a Christian. There is the body made new in the spirit, (Ephesians 4:24) and there is the body not made new, which is our flesh. It is this natural, outer shell that gets attacked by evil, and never the spiritual body. It is a distinction between the sanctification of our spirits versus the sanctification of our flesh. The sanctification of the spirit means our spirits have been made new by Christ and are no longer slaves to our sinful natures. Our spirits are sealed by the Holy Spirit, and can in no way be touched by the enemy. They belong to God, and we have this as a guarantee.

Now He who establishes us with you in Christ and has anointed us is God, who also has sealed us and given us the Spirit in our hearts as a guarantee. (2 Corinthians 1:21–22)

The body of the "flesh," however, has not been "born again," and is still dust destined to return to the ground.

> "...For dust you are, And to dust you shall return." (Genesis 3:19)

The Bible makes the distinction between these two bodies very clear.

> "That which is born of the flesh is flesh, and that which is born of the Spirit is spirit." (John 3:6)

There is even an enormous struggle going on between these two natures within us. The spiritual body is holy and desires to live accordingly to the ways of God, while our natural body is sinful, seeking its own fleshly desires.

> I say then: Walk in the Spirit, and you shall not fulfill the lust of the flesh. For the flesh lusts against the Spirit, and the Spirit against the flesh; and these are contrary to one another, so that you do not do the things that you wish. But if you are led by the Spirit, you are not under the law. Now the works of the flesh are evident, which are: adultery, fornication, uncleanness, lewdness, idolatry, sorcery, hatred, contentions, jealousies, outbursts of wrath, selfish ambitions, dissensions, heresies, envy, murders, drunkenness, revelries, and the like; of which I tell you beforehand, just as I also told you in time past, that those who practice such things will not inherit the kingdom of God. But the fruit of the Spirit is love, joy, peace, longsuffering, kindness, goodness, faithfulness, gentleness, self-control. Against such there is no law. And those who are Christ's have crucified the flesh with its passions and desires. If we live in the Spirit, let us also walk in the Spirit. Let us not become conceited, provoking one another, envying one another. (Galatians 5:16–26)

Even Paul, an extraordinarily strong Christian, proclaimed the difference between his spirit and his fleshly body.

> O wretched man that I am! Who will deliver me from this body of death? I thank God-through Jesus Christ our Lord!

So then, with the mind I myself serve the law of God, but with the flesh the law of sin. (Romans 7:24–25)

It is this "wretched" body where sin dwells and evil inhabits. This makes perfect sense. As sin is evil, and able to dwell within us, so sickness, caused by evil, is able to dwell within us.

Sin gives opportunity for evil to enter, and this is one of the reasons the Bible admonishes us to walk according to the spirit and never to give an opportunity to the devil.

"Be angry and do not sin: do not let the sun go down on your wrath, not give place to the devil." (Ephesians 4:26–27)

Because the carnal mind is enmity against God; for it is not subject to the law of God, nor indeed can be. So then, those who are in the flesh cannot please God. (Romans 8:7–8)

When we as believers confess our sins to Jesus Christ, we are forgiven and cleansed from all unrighteousness.

If we confess our sins, He is faithful and just to forgive us our sins and to cleanse us from all unrighteousness. (1 John 1:9)

The devil has no power to control or make Christians do anything because we are no longer slaves to sin. He can only tempt us to follow our sinful desires. It is ultimately our disobedience that brings danger. If we lived in absolute obedience to Christ upon receiving forgiveness and never sinned, evil would be unable to dwell in the body. There would be no opening for them to enter. The unfortunate reality is that we as Christians all fall down in the weakness of our flesh and give evil opportunity.

This same situation existed in the Garden of Eden. Satan had no authority over Adam and Even until they sinned and were separated from God. Sin in our lives breaks perfect unity with the Father. Thank God that today we can immediately confess our sin, stand strong in His forgiveness, and remove the spiritual enemies causing destruction. Thank God that Jesus has not only provided a way for us to be forgiven, but also a way for our physical bodies to be delivered from the power of the enemy.

They Come Back

Another difficult question to answer for those who believe that unclean spirits cannot enter a Christian's body, is how they are able to return to the body from which they were sent out of. If demons can only reside in the unsaved, and are cast out of a person who just became a Christian (those freed from the power of the enemy), they would never be able to enter again. The Bible teaches that we should never take our eyes off the enemy because they will try to come back to the home they were cast out of.

> **"When an unclean spirit goes out of a man, he goes through dry places, seeking rest; and finding none, he says, 'I will return to my house from which I came.' And when he comes, he finds it swept and put in order. Then he goes and takes with him seven other spirits more wicked than himself, and they enter and dwell there; and the last state of that man is worse than the first." (Luke 11:24–26)**

This is one of the reasons that the devil's army works so hard tempting us to sin. Unclean spirits desire to get back in because they seek "rest" in our bodies. Look again at the man who was just healed by Jesus and told to sin no more lest a worse thing come upon him.

> **In these lay a great multitude of sick people, blind, lame, paralyzed, waiting for the moving of the water. For an angel went down at a certain time into the pool and stirred up the water; then whoever stepped in first, after the stirring of the water, was made well of whatever disease he had. Now a certain man was there who had an infirmity thirty-eight years. When Jesus saw him lying there, and knew that he already had been in that condition a long time, He said to him, "Do you want to be made well?" The sick man answered Him, "Sir, I have no man to put me into the pool when the water is stirred up; but while I am coming, another steps down before me." Jesus said to him, "Rise, take up your bed and walk." And immediately the man was made well, took up his bed, and walked. And that day was the Sabbath. The Jews therefore said to him who**

was cured, "It is the Sabbath; it is not lawful for you to carry your bed." He answered them, "He who made me well said to me, 'Take up your bed and walk.'" Then they asked him, "Who is the Man who said to you, 'Take up your bed and walk'?" But the one who was healed did not know who it was, for Jesus had withdrawn, a multitude being in that place. Afterward Jesus found him in the temple, and said to him, "See, you have been made well. Sin no more, lest a worse thing come upon you." The man departed and told the Jews that it was Jesus who had made him well. (John 5:3–15)

An Undeniable Fact

The difference between theory and reality is the degree of certainty we can assign to information as being true. Given the best way to validate information is by witnessing its effect or evidence, we can have the utmost confidence that the Bible's teaching is true. Christians strong in their faith are plagued with every kind of sickness, disease, and trouble just as the rest of the world. When they learn of their enemy, and pray for Jesus to remove them, they are healed! They addressed the root of the problem, stood strong in the power of Jesus Christ, and received the blessing! This is direct fulfillment and confirmation of God's promise. (Please see chapter 13 for many documented examples.)

"...wisdom is justified by her children." (Matthew 11:19)

We know this instruction to be true because of the fruit it bears. Great evidence is witnessed during prayer that evil spirits inhabit our bodies, but greater evidence is the fact that the sickness and problems leave!

The first lie Satan attempts to deceive you with is that he doesn't exist. If that doesn't work, he goes further trying to get you to believe he doesn't exist in your life! Satan's worst nightmare is a faith-filled Christian on his/her knees armed with an understanding of his wiles, and how to overcome them in Christ's power.

And He said to them, "Go into all the world and preach the gospel to every creature. He who believes and is baptized

will be saved; but he who does not believe will be condemned. And these signs will follow those who believe: In
My name they will cast out demons; they will speak with
new tongues; they will take up serpents; and if they drink
anything deadly, it will by no means hurt them; they will
lay hands on the sick, and they will recover." So then, after
the Lord had spoken to them, He was received up into
heaven, and sat down at the right hand of God. And they
went out and preached everywhere, the Lord working with
them and confirming the word through the accompanying
signs. Amen. (Mark 16:15–20)

These signs have been produced by the Lord "working" and "confirming" His word among those who believe in His promise. Lay
aside the devil's deceptions and wage the warfare to which we have
all been called. Stand strong in the power and might of the Lord
and overcome all the power of the enemy in your life! (Chapter 14
covers a detailed description of how to accomplish this.)

TESTIMONY: Brad Walker
Birth Date: July 14, 1966
Occupation: Project Manager
Experience: **Healed of tonsillitis**
Date of Testimony: June 1, 1997

Since March of this year (1997) my throat has been bothering me constantly. It started as a minor sore throat, became a severe sore throat, and finally developed into tonsillitis. I went to the doctor and he prescribed penicillin for ten days. After each set, my throat no longer hurt, but I would still have problems swallowing, and my throat would begin hurting again. Over the next three months, I went to three different doctors receiving no relief. I would miss Tae Kwon Do class because I was very weak, lost a lot of weight, and had no energy. I continued to go to the doctors, but always got contradicting opinions. One doctor recommended I should have my tonsils removed, while another doctor recommended against it.

Master Kim encouraged me to speak with him, and told me that I could be healed. Though I continued to miss class, and was not able to meet, he continued to call my house, and leave messages. Finally, I met with him last week after suffering for three months. He showed me the Bible, and we read different passages all with the same meaning. Jesus Christ died for us and his blood washed away all of our sins. He promised us a life full of joy and without sickness. We then proceeded to pray together. Master Kim put his hands on my head and prayed to cast out the demons that were hurting me for so long. Following our prayer, I no longer felt any pain, my throat didn't hurt, and I had no trouble swallowing. Master Kim opened my eyes to God, and I will never forget this experience. I now read the Bible on a daily basis, and will go to church to pray for my family and yours.

Chapter XII
A Mighty Call to Battle

Now that we have covered the creation of mankind, the nature of our enemy, and God's promise of freedom, we must learn more of our position in Jesus Christ, along with the tremendous authority we have in His name!

When Jesus Christ physically walked the earth he chose 12 very average men to spend time with. One of the reasons was to train them to do what He was doing! Jesus knew that He was going to hang on a cross, die, and eventually rise to the right hand of the Father in heaven. Consequently, Jesus wanted these men to understand their new position in the world, and how to use the power He would send them. The disciples did not understand the true meaning of Jesus' death until after His resurrection. Their hearts were initially broken when they saw the beaten and bloodied body of Jesus hanging dead on the cross. They not only thought they lost their friend and teacher, but also their very hope. We see this in the Gospel of Luke when two men explained their feelings after Jesus' death.

> **"But we were hoping that it was He who was going to redeem Israel. Indeed besides all this, today is the third day since these things happened." (Luke 24:21)**

The disciples forgot that Jesus promised He was going to send power to them, and did not understand they were called to continue His work. Listen to Jesus as He prays to God the Father about a believer's position in the world. God has prepared everything for us to live and work in His power!

> "Now I am no longer in the world, but these are in the world, and I come to You. Holy Father, keep through Your name those whom You have given Me, that they may be one as We are. While I was with them in the world, I kept them in Your name. Those whom You gave Me I have kept; and none of them is lost except the son of perdition, that the Scripture might be fulfilled. But now I come to You, and these things I speak in the world, that they may have My joy fulfilled in themselves. I have given them Your word; and the world has hated them because they are not of the world, just as I am not of the world. I do not pray that You should take them out of the world, but that You should keep them from the evil one. They are not of the world, just as I am not of the world. Sanctify them by Your truth. Your word is truth. As You sent Me into the world, I also have sent them into the world. And for their sakes I sanctify Myself, that they also may be sanctified by the truth. I do not pray for these alone, but also for those who will believe in Me through their word; that they all may be one, as You, Father, are in Me, and I in You; that they also may be one in Us, that the world may believe that You sent Me. And the glory which You gave Me I have given them, that they may be one just as We are one: I in them, and You in Me; that they may be made perfect in one, and that the world may know that You have sent Me, and have loved them as You have loved Me. Father, I desire that they also whom You gave Me may be with Me where I am, that they may behold My glory which You have given Me; for You loved Me before the foundation of the world. O righteous Father! The world has not known You, but I have known You; and these have known that You sent Me. And I have declared to them Your name, and will declare it, that the love with which You loved Me may be in them, and I in them." (John 17:11–26)

Here we see that Jesus knows He will no longer be in the world, but we will continue to be. *"Now I am no longer in the world, but these are in the world, and I come to You."* (John 17:11) Then we see that Jesus

prays for us not to be taken out of the world, but that we are protected from the evil one. *"I do not pray that You should take them out of
the world, but that You should keep them from the evil one."* (John 17:15)
Next, we can see that our position as believers in Jesus Christ is
very different than most people have realized. *"As You sent Me into
the world, I also have sent them into the world."* (John 17:18)

We are sent and privileged to continue the works of Jesus in
the world! Not the work of dying on the cross for sins, for only Jesus
could have accomplished that, but rather to preach the Kingdom of
God and administer God's gift to free all those in bondage to the
devil. God knows the impossibility of us continuing His work in
our own strength, and, therefore, sent the gift of the Holy Spirit. He
is the third person of the triune God (trinity) and is the Spirit of God
who dwells in the believers of Jesus Christ. The Holy Spirit enables
us to do the work of God because He is working within us. He gives
power to stand strong in Jesus Christ and successfully resist the devil.
Jesus, when speaking to the disciples, said,

> So Jesus said to them again, "Peace to you! As the Father
> has sent Me, I also send you." And when He had said this,
> He breathed on them, and said to them, "Receive the Holy
> Spirit." (John 20:21–22)

> "But you shall receive power when the Holy Spirit has come
> upon you; and you shall be witnesses to Me in Jerusalem,
> and in all Judea and Samaria, and to the end of the earth."
> (Acts 1:8)

> "If you love Me, keep My commandments. And I will pray
> the Father, and He will give you another Helper, that He
> may abide with you forever—the Spirit of truth, whom the
> world cannot receive, because it neither sees Him nor knows
> Him; but you know Him, for He dwells with you and will
> be in you. I will not leave you orphans; I will come to you."
> (John 14:15–18)

It is critical to understand that there is no difference between
us and the disciples in the Bible. Not one of them had any power
without Jesus first giving it to them. The wonderful truth is that

Jesus not only gave power to the 12 disciples, but has also given power to all those who believe in Him. This is how we can continue His work and accomplish His will. Believe it or not, when you have the power of God living inside of you, you can do what Jesus did, and even greater!

> "Most assuredly, I say to you, he who believes in Me, the works that I do he will do also; and greater works than these he will do, because I go to My Father. And whatever you ask in My name, that I will do, that the Father may be glorified in the Son. If you ask anything in My name, I will do it." (John 14:12–14)

If you grasp the meaning of this verse, it will change life as you know it. Jesus is literally telling every believer that we can do whatever He did, and even greater, because He has gone to the Father. Yes! Jesus has given power and authority to do great and mighty works in His name. If you believe, you have power to overcome *all* the power of the enemy so that you can be healed of every sickness, disease, and weakness! Nothing can hurt you! Listen to Jesus' words.

> And He said to them, "I saw Satan fall like lightning from heaven. Behold, I give you the authority to trample on serpents and scorpions, and over all the power of the enemy, and nothing shall by any means hurt you. Nevertheless do not rejoice in this, that the spirits are subject to you, but rather rejoice because your names are written in heaven." (Luke 10:18–20)

Don't allow the devil to keep you in bondage any longer. We are called to use the power that Christ has provided for us to break free! We must answer this call to action exactly as the believers did in the Bible. Let's look at some examples of Jesus Christ specifically telling His followers to act with His power and authority.

> And when He had called His twelve disciples to Him, He gave them power over unclean spirits, to cast them out, and to heal all kinds of sickness and all kinds of disease. (Matthew 10:1)

> Then He appointed twelve, that they might be with Him and that He might send them out to preach, and to have power to heal sicknesses and to cast out demons. (Mark 3:14–15)

> And He called the twelve to Himself, and began to send them out two by two, and gave them power over unclean spirits. (Mark 6:7)

These believers never worked in their own strength, but were *given* power for the working of His will and promises. Notice this power was inclusive over *all* the power of the enemy (Luke 10:19), leaving no doubt that we can overcome every trial or tribulation caused by the devil.

> Then He called His twelve disciples together and gave them power and authority over all demons, and to cure diseases. He sent them to preach the kingdom of God and to heal the sick. (Luke 9:1–2)

> "And as you go, preach, saying, 'The kingdom of heaven is at hand.' Heal the sick, cleanse the lepers, raise the dead, cast out demons. Freely you have received, freely give." (Matthew 10:7–8)

Jesus *"commanded"* them to heal the sick, cleanse the lepers, raise the dead, and cast out demons. As children of Jesus Christ, we *must* be at work for the Kingdom of God. If God has given us power to use, then we must use it—not only for our own benefit, but also for God's glory. Accordingly, the disciples preached the Kingdom of God, healed the sick, and demonstrated that Jesus Christ was truly the Son of God.

> So they departed and went through the towns, preaching the gospel and healing everywhere. (Luke 9:6)

Shortly after receiving the Holy Spirit, Peter and John (disciples of Jesus) saw a crippled man asking for money. Peter and John had the power of Jesus Christ in them, and they used this power and authority in the name of Jesus Christ to heal the man.

> Now Peter and John went up together to the temple at the hour of prayer, the ninth hour. And a certain man lame from his mother's womb was carried, whom they laid daily at the gate of the temple which is called Beautiful, to ask alms from those who entered the temple who, seeing Peter and John about to go into the temple, asked for alms. And fixing his eyes on him, with John, Peter said, "Look at us." So he gave them his attention, expecting to receive something from them. Then Peter said, "Silver and gold I do not have, but what I do have I give you: In the name of Jesus Christ of Nazareth, rise up and walk." And he took him by the right hand and lifted him up, and immediately his feet and anklebones received strength. So he, leaping up, stood and walked and entered the temple with them—walking, leaping, and praising God. And all the people saw him walking and praising God. Then they knew that it was he who sat begging alms at the Beautiful Gate of the temple; and they were filled with wonder and amazement at what had happened to him. (Acts 3:1–10)

This was not Peter's power. It was the promise of Jesus Christ working through Peter.

Let's look at another situation when Paul was shipwrecked on an island called Malta. As Paul was staying there, the father of a leading citizen of the island was sick with a fever. Paul went and prayed with him, and the power of Jesus Christ worked through Paul to heal him.

> And it happened that the father of Publius lay sick of a fever and dysentery. Paul went in to him and prayed, and he laid his hands on him and healed him. So when this was done, the rest of those on the island who had diseases also came and were healed. (Acts 28:8–9)

Paul didn't just pray with the father of Publius to help him deal with the pain. He went to bring the promise of God that was entrusted to him, and the man was healed! The results were astounding! The rest of those on the island who had diseases also came and were healed. A tremendous effect of obeying God's command to use His power is that others come to know that Jesus is the only Son of God and are freed from the power of the enemy.

Another instance occurred when Philip went down to the city of Samaria to share the Gospel of Jesus.

> **Then Philip went down to the city of Samaria and preached Christ to them. And the multitudes with one accord heeded the things spoken by Philip, hearing and seeing the miracles, which he did. For unclean spirits, crying with a loud voice, came out of many who were possessed; and many who were paralyzed and lame were healed. And there was great joy in that city. (Acts 8:5–8)**

Another example occurred when Peter went to a town called Lydda, where he found a man who had been in bed for eight years because he was paralyzed.

> **There he found a certain man named Aeneas, who had been bedridden eight years and was paralyzed. And Peter said to him, "Aeneas, Jesus the Christ heals you. Arise and make your bed." Then he arose immediately. So all who dwelt at Lydda and Sharon saw him and turned to the Lord. (Acts 9:33–35)**

Notice the scripture says Jesus the Christ healed the man. Peter was an instrument of God, used the power and authority given to him, and the crippled man walked! These are all examples of Jesus Christ imparting His power and authority to believers for the accomplishment of His work.

Power Can Be Yours!

Some believe God only gave power to cast out demons and work miracles to the 12 disciples. Nothing could be further from the truth! The 12 disciples were only the first to be trained. Jesus needed to train many more because the harvest is great in size, and the workers are so few.

> **After these things the Lord appointed seventy others also, and sent them two by two before His face into every city and place where He Himself was about to go. Then He said to them, "The harvest truly is great, but the laborers**

are few; therefore pray the Lord of the harvest to send out laborers into His harvest. Go your way; behold, I send you out as lambs among wolves. Carry neither money bag, knapsack, nor sandals; and greet no one along the road. But whatever house you enter, first say, 'Peace to this house.' And if a son of peace is there, your peace will rest on it; if not, it will return to you. And remain in the same house, eating and drinking such things as they give, for the laborer is worthy of his wages. Do not go from house to house. Whatever city you enter, and they receive you, eat such things as are set before you. And heal the sick there, and say to them, 'The kingdom of God has come near to you.'" (Luke 10:1–9)

After the 12 disciples, God sent out an additional 70 men to do His work of healing the sick. Jesus Christ grants His power and authority to every one of His children, not just a select few!

Then the seventy returned with joy, saying, "Lord, even the demons are subject to us in Your name." And He said to them, "I saw Satan fall like lightning from heaven. Behold, I give you the authority to trample on serpents and scorpions, and over all the power of the enemy, and nothing shall by any means hurt you. Nevertheless do not rejoice in this, that the spirits are subject to you, but rather rejoice because your names are written in heaven." (Luke 10:17–20)

These 70 men did what Jesus commanded them, and they returned reporting that demons obeyed them in front of the *name of Jesus Christ*! Jesus is saying to us...

"Behold, I give you the authority to trample on serpents and scorpions, and over all the power of the enemy, and nothing shall by any means hurt you." (Luke 10:19)

You have been given the power to overcome the wiles of the devil because you are a child of God. There is no random selection of a specially chosen few who can live in the power and might of Jesus' strength. We are all attacked by the devil, and all need Jesus' power to stand strong and overcome. Regardless of your individual circumstance, rest assured that Jesus not only wants you to break free, but has given you the power to do it!

> "Most assuredly, I say to you, he who believes in Me, the works that I do he will do also; and greater works than these he will do, because I go to My Father. And whatever you ask in My name, that I will do, that the Father may be glorified in the Son. If you ask anything in My name, I will do it." (John 14:12–14)

The difference between these disciples and many of us is that we don't act in God's power. We talk about it, we study it, we scrutinize over it, but we don't often put it into action. Move in faith and His power will flow. Speak the word of God aloud when it says,

> I can do all things through Christ who strengthens me. (Philippians 4:13)

The Mighty Power of His Name

The fact that you know God has provided power to each believer to work miracles and to cast out demons isn't enough to break free. We must understand how to stand strong in His power, and how to put this knowledge into practice. Let's look again at Peter and the healing of the crippled man.

> Now Peter and John went up together to the temple at the hour of prayer, the ninth hour. And a certain man lame from his mother's womb was carried, whom they laid daily at the gate of the temple which is called Beautiful, to ask alms from those who entered the temple who, seeing Peter and John about to go into the temple, asked for alms. And fixing his eyes on him, with John, Peter said, "Look at us." So he gave them his attention, expecting to receive something from them. Then Peter said, "Silver and gold I do not have, but what I do have I give you: In the name of Jesus Christ of Nazareth, rise up and walk." And he took him by the right hand and lifted him up, and immediately his feet and anklebones received strength. So he, leaping up, stood and

walked and entered the temple with them—walking, leaping, and praising God. And all the people saw him walking and praising God. Then they knew that it was he who sat begging alms at the Beautiful Gate of the temple; and they were filled with wonder and amazement at what had happened to him. (Acts 3:1–10)

Peter specifically said, *"In the name of Jesus Christ of Nazareth, rise up and walk."* (Acts 3:6) It was the name of Jesus Christ which enabled access to His power and authority. Not only the name, however, but faith in His name. We see this point clearly communicated.

"And His name, through faith in His name, has made this man strong, whom you see and know. Yes, the faith which comes through Him has given him this perfect soundness in the presence of you all." (Acts 3:16)

"...let it be known to you all, and to all the people of Israel, that by the name of Jesus Christ of Nazareth, whom you crucified, whom God raised from the dead, by Him this man stands here before you whole." (Acts 4:10)

Satan knows the name of Jesus Christ brings defeat to him and his entire army. This is why Satan worked through unbelieving men attempting to stop believers from speaking in the name of Jesus Christ.

Now when they saw the boldness of Peter and John, and perceived that they were uneducated and untrained men, they marveled. And they realized that they had been with Jesus. And seeing the man who had been healed standing with them, they could say nothing against it. But when they had commanded them to go aside out of the council, they conferred among themselves, saying, "What shall we do to these men? For, indeed, that a notable miracle has been done through them is evident to all who dwell in Jerusalem, and we cannot deny it. But so that it spreads no further among the people, let us severely threaten them, that from now on they speak to no man in this name." And they called them and commanded them not to speak at all nor teach in the name of Jesus. But Peter and John answered and said to them, "Whether it is right in the sight of God to

listen to you more than to God, you judge. For we cannot but speak the things which we have seen and heard." So when they had further threatened them, they let them go, finding no way of punishing them, because of the people, since they all glorified God for what had been done. For the man was over forty years old on whom this miracle of healing had been performed. And being let go, they went to their own companions and reported all that the chief priests and elders had said to them. (Acts 4:13–23)

These men of God were fearless and remained bold praying for God to continue to work miracles through His *name*.

"Now, Lord, look on their threats, and grant to Your servants that with all boldness they may speak Your word, by stretching out Your hand to heal, and that signs and wonders may be done through the name of Your holy Servant Jesus." (Acts 4:29–30)

God's Power Is Still Working Through Us!

Read the following accounts in chapter 13 about how people overcame their sicknesses, problems, and weaknesses by accepting Jesus Christ as their Savior, and casting out demons in His name. Read carefully, and you will see the word of God is still living and powerful in our lives today. You too will receive the blessings of God in the name of Jesus Christ exactly as these people when you act in faith on His Word. Additional testimonies can be found in the back of the book.

TESTIMONY: Jackie Adams
Birth Date: September 17, 1968
Occupation: Marketing Manager
Experience: **Healed from hypoglycemia**
Date of Testimony: June 4, 2001

In January 2001 I had started feeling rather ill. An unexplain-able overall feeling of fatigue, weakness, disorientation, and anxiety. I didn't know what was happening, I only knew it was getting worse. In February, I had what someone called a "panic attack" while relaxing with my father (my best buddy) on the couch. I couldn't understand why I would have had a panic attack while I was enjoying myself...it made no sense. But the attack was horrible! I thought I was dying. I couldn't see, my heart was racing, my hands and feet went numb, and I began to shake all over. Periodically, I would encounter less pronounced episodes, but one day while at work, I had an awful attack. I was sent to the emergency room, and after several tests and doctor visits, I was officially diagnosed with hypoglycemia in April 2001. I prayed, but it still lingered. I couldn't eat any of the foods that I enjoyed, and I was in total bondage. I would fear having an attack so much that it practically paralyzed me. I wouldn't go to any events that might have precluded me from getting food or juice in a hurry. I wouldn't go anywhere that would throw me off my "eating schedule." I didn't eat any ice cream or treats, and I stopped baking, which is one of my fa-vorite hobbies. I was in a word, MISERABLE. Then, I visited my friends Steve and Kate and learned again what I knew, but had trouble acting on...that I was already healed by the blood of Christ. He took my hypoglycemia and anything else you want to call it almost 2,000 years ago when he died for me on the cross. I am not meant to have illness or pain. I am not meant to suffer and live in bondage. That is NOT the will of God for my life. He died to give me life, and give it to me in abundance. What I was living was not anything like His will. It was Satan's will to hurt me. After a night of reading scripture, and affirming my position as a child of God Almighty, a daughter, a treasure in His eyes, I believed, I had faith, I trusted. Steve and my friends prayed for me, and I was fully healed! I am able to eat when I want, and what I want, and I'm out of that horrible bondage. On occasion, I fall under attack, but I pray, and it immediately leaves me. I thank God for His merciful healing and grace.

Chapter XIII
Amazing Stories: God's Word Proven

Many of these testimonies reference the authors of this book, Dong Jin Kim and Steve Hannett, but please note we hold no special power different from any other believer. We are simply followers of Jesus Christ and are acting on His promises. Jesus Christ is the one who deserves all of the honor and glory. It is Jesus who healed all these people, and Jesus who has changed their lives forever. These true stories prove that God wants to bless, and these few examples are only a sampling of the many amazing testimonies received during more than 20 years of ministry. Please note that some names have been changed for reasons of confidentiality.

#1: Cathy Yang
Occupation: Accountant
Experience: **Healed from asthma**
Date of Testimony: February 26, 2002

I have struggled with asthma since childhood and was constantly sick when I was growing up. I watched my health very carefully, and my sickness gradually went away as I reached adulthood. Eventually, I became healthy and asthma free.

Even though I am fully aware of my allergic reaction to certain animals, I took in my first cat six years ago. The antigen from cat dander triggered a recurrence of asthmatic reactions. For four years, I received allergy injections, on a weekly basis. During that time, I visited numerous pulmonary specialists, and was in the emergency room twice from acute attacks. I have used most of the medications on the market, and have relied on steroids, inhalers, and a nebulizer. Shortly after I began attending Grand Master Kim's Blue Dragon Tae Kwon Do Academy in August 2001, he became aware of my afflictions. Then Grand Master Kim talked with me about spiritual development and the power of Jesus Christ. He explained to me that if I believed in God's love, Jesus Christ could work through him and that He could rid me of asthma. At the end of the second spiritual session, Grand Master Kim started to pray to God. He laid his palm on top of my head, and repeatedly commanded the evil spirit to get out of my body, continuing for over forty minutes. I could feel his powerful voice and sensed a lot of energy in the room. After that, the asthma attacks gradually lessened in severity and eventually stopped! I no longer wheeze, and my breathing has improved tremendously. For the first time, I can leave home without my inhaler! I will always be extremely grateful to Jesus Christ for healing me, and for Grand Master Kim's dedication to helping people.

#2: Lawrence Koester
Birth Date: February 21, 1985
Occupation: Student
Experience: **Healed of cancer and motion sickness**
Date of Testimony: September 15, 1999

July 1999 is when all my problems started. I couldn't bend my leg because my knee was hurting a lot. I told Master Kim about it and he said to pray to the Lord every day. In the beginning, I really didn't believe that my knee would heal if I prayed to God. Two weeks went by, and for no reason I started to vomit every day. I just kept it to myself and thought that it would go away if I gave my body some time to heal. A few more weeks passed by, and I was still vomiting every day. Also, whenever I rode a car, train, or bus, I wouldn't be able to breathe. So I finally told Master Kim and he told me that I was being controlled by demons. I heard about the demons from him before, but the problem was that I never really believed. Master Kim prayed for me. After about ten minutes, I actually saw the demons myself. There were more than a thousand demons in me. I definitely knew that I had cancer, but not anymore. Thanks to Jesus Christ I was saved. The kingdom of heaven came to me. I always have the Lord next to me and nothing will stop me from reading the Bible. I am thankful the demons are out of me, and glad that the Lord is always with me.

#3: Bruce Malley
Birth Date: July 9, 1954
Occupation: Postal Worker
Experience: **Healed of a knee and back injury and tendonitis**
Date of Testimony: March 14, 1997

On June 23, 1995, I met Master Kim through a friend of mine who gave my son Steven six months of tae kwon do classes for his birthday. As time passed, Master Kim and I became friends. Master Kim would always tell me I should become more flexible, so in June of 1997 I started classes myself. When I would come to class, we would talk about my son, family, and life in general. I would tell him about the pain in my left knee I had for the past few years, my back pain from a car accident, and my tendonitis I developed from weightlifting in 1991.

Over time we started talking more and more about God and the powers of healing. So on March 14, 1997, Master Kim said he would help my pain. We read the Bible, talked about God's healing power and what it all meant. Master Kim said just to believe in God and that He would help me. So Master Kim and I started to pray. When I stood up, Master Kim put his hands on the sides of my head and started asking God to cast the demons from my body. As he was praying, I felt numb, like I was in a daze. It was like I was there with him, but I wasn't. I could hear him, but couldn't move, and I felt like I was somewhere else. When Master Kim was finished, the demons left my body.

When it was all over I felt at ease, and a calm came over me like I never had before. I thanked God and left. That Sunday after church 3-16-97, I ran three miles with no problems, on Monday 3-17-97 in class I did 100 pushups with no pain, and on Tuesday 3-18-97 I ran another two miles, then lifted weights with a friend with no pain. I guess this all means if you believe in God, He will help you.

#4: Bruce Malley
Birth Date: July 9, 1954
Occupation: Postal Worker
Experience: **Healed from headache**
Date of Testimony: October 23, 1998

On Tuesday 10-20-98, I came down with an extremely painful headache, my head was pounding, my eyes hurt, and I felt as if I was going to vomit. I worked all night in pain without medication. The next morning 10-21-98, Wednesday, I came home from work and went to bed. That afternoon I went to the gym hoping it would go away, but it didn't. I even took an aspirin with no help. So at 5:30 PM I took my son to class and spoke to Master Kim. He told me not to worry, just to ask Jesus for help because demons were making me sick. While praying, I felt an energy flow through my body, my breathing became slow and deep, then my head dropped down. I felt relaxed and calm. Master Kim laid me on the floor put his hand on my forehead and prayed a little more. After that I felt relieved of any pain or discomfort. Master Kim and I talked a little after we were done. I said I felt fine and took my seven o'clock class. I guess what this all means is if you live a clean life, and believe in Jesus, you will be saved and protected from the demons that try to destroy our lives.

#5: Kevin Vick
Birth Date: December 15, 1958
Occupation: Postal Clerk
Experience: **Healed of a degenerative spinal condition**
Date of Testimony: July 14, 1997

In February of 1997, I was getting ready to go to work as usual. On my way downstairs, I realized I had forgotten my work keys. I started back up the stairs and suddenly felt a sharp pain in my lower back. The pain bothered me somewhat, but it wasn't severe enough to keep me home from work. That night the pain was still present so I took Advil and put on a heating pad. When I awoke the next day, I could hardly move my back and it was spasming even when I lay still. I could not get up or walk without assistance. My wife called my doctor and took me to see him that same day. I needed a "walker" to lean on to get into the office. The doctor prescribed Valium Tylox (painkiller) and an anti-inflammatory. I was told to return in one week. After the week had passed with little improvement, I was sent for an MRI, still on the same medications. The MRI revealed a degenerative disc disease present with a narrowing of the spinal cord canal and multiple bone spurs. I was told by my doctor it was inoperable and only treatable by medication therapy.

My symptoms lessened to a degree, where I was able to move and walk on my own, but the pain persisted. The drugs I was given to help me caused me to become ill. I experienced severe nausea and leg cramps at night. I decided I had to live with the pain. I already was taking multiple medications for my chronic asthma and sinusitis, and these pain managers were just not helping.

Shortly after my back incident, my daughter enrolled in Master Kim's Tae Kwon Do School. My wife came home one day after class and told me she knew someone who could help her with her arthritis and my back disease/arthritis. She asked if I was interested in having my back taken care of, and I said, "Yes". When she told me later that the person who would help us was Master Kim, I was surprised and skeptical. I thought to myself that it must be some kind of acupuncture or herbal therapy. As the day of our scheduled meeting drew closer, Master Kim kept reassuring me it would be a great day.

When my wife and I met with Master Kim, we were both shocked when he had us read the testimonies of people who had been healed. Master Kim then took out a Bible and had me read selected passages. I told Master Kim while I was reading, I felt a fluttering or beating in my chest. I continued to read and still felt the fluttering. I started to feel very excited and slightly scared. When we were done reading, Master Kim, my wife, another gentlemen, and myself went to pray. He then told me to stand up. I stood and he placed his hands on my head, and told me to look at him. I did this and he began to look deep inside me and began speaking to me (mostly in Korean, I believe). I assumed he was praying and casting the demons out of me, which he told me were responsible for my ailments. While he was still praying, I began to feel my eyes fluttering and spasms were coming over my facial muscles. There was nothing amusing about what was going on and yet, I nearly felt like laughing. After a few minutes, Master Kim gripped my head firmly and told me to lie down. I felt lighter and more peaceful than I ever remembered feeling before. He told me to lie still, I didn't know what else to do but pray. I prayed to myself over and over "Christ is my Savior." While I was lying there praying, Master Kim prayed for my wife also, and she was also healed.

My back problem no longer exists, and my asthma is much more under control with less and less medication being used. Master Kim advised us to read the Bible, go to church, and find a good pastor. We have both been awakened to the spirit, and

I personally can feel it growing stronger daily as I myself am growing stronger. I believe that I was healed by God through Master Kim in the name of Jesus Christ. I now look at life more positively and hopefully. I know the future will be better for me thanks in no small part to my personal relationship with Jesus Christ.

#6: Marissa Wegman
Birth Date: August 9, 1970
Occupation: Printing Production
Experience: **Healed of stress attacks and body pain**
Date of Testimony: Not recorded

I have been married a little over a year, and was starting to constantly fight all the time. I became totally irrational and was never happy anymore. I knew that my way of thinking and my decisions started to become more and more unlike me. When I summed up all of these changes, I realized I was losing control of myself. I wanted everything in my life to just stop so I could take a step back and look at everything that was going on. I came back to Master Kim's classes after four years. I started to feel a little bit better about myself but not enough. I looked forward to his Saturday classes, but on this one particular morning (the day before Palm Sunday) I had such a stress attack on my way to work, that by the time I got to work, I couldn't even turn my head. Everything hurt. That day I realized that all of these evil things (confusion, pain, etc.) were taking over me. All I wanted to do was stop the pain, curl up in a ball, and cry. Instead, I showed up at Master Kim's school but not for class. Somehow I knew he would help me, and he did. He prayed for me, and he prayed with me. He forced all evil out of me and along with them went the pain in my heart that was never meant to be there. The next day I forced myself to run for a little while and before I even realized it, my body wasn't in pain anymore. That morning I also went to church. I feel that my faith in God is what healed me. Just like we need to discipline ourselves to practice Karate, we need to condition our minds and spirits also.

#7: Tammy Zapallo
Birth Date: June 5, 1961
Occupation: Registered Nurse
Experience: **Healed of swollen glands, canker sores, and thumb infection**
Date of Testimony: August 9, 1997

I went to see Master D.J. Kim on Monday, August 4, 1997, because I was afflicted with canker sores in my mouth, swollen glands, and an infection in my right thumb. I felt weak and I was unable to eat. I had visited the doctor who gave me antibiotics several days before, and cut open my finger to drain the infection, but I was feeling worse. The doctor said that I was under stress and unable to fight the infection. Master Kim prayed for me and explained passages from the Bible to me. Then he cast out a demon from my body. I immediately felt at peace and felt some relief of my discomfort. I went home and I was able to eat for the first time in several days. By the next day I felt much stronger and was able to take my Tae Kwon Do class. On Wednesday, August 6, 1997, I started to feel more discomfort again. I was unable to eat, the sores spread in my mouth, I had a fever and my finger was throbbing with pain. I was unable to sleep. Again the doctors drained my finger with no relief. I went to Master Kim on Thursday, August 7, 1997, before my Tae Kwon Do class. Master Kim prayed for me again and cast out a demon and told me to make sure to pray. By Friday, August 8, 1997, I was strong in my arm, and my right thumb felt better. The sores in my mouth were almost gone. I felt strong enough to take my Tae Kwon Do Orange Belt test that day which I didn't take a few days earlier. I prayed and read the Bible, and I still feel strong with a clearer mind and decreased stress.

#8: Daniel Bryer
Birth Date: July 11, 1959
Occupation: Computer Operator
Experience: **Chronic back pain and mental problems**
Date of Testimony: April 13, 1995

My problems began about six years ago. I was suffering from chronic back pain. As a student of Master Kim's, I was helped through the healing of Jesus Christ. I have been helped as many as 25 times throughout the six years. I believe through faith in Jesus Christ, all good things come. After being healed, I felt a lifting of a cloud that had burdened me. I felt relieved to know that through the power of Jesus Christ, evil spirits are cast out. Today as I write this April 13, 1995, I was helped again. I had a problem with demons in my mind. After we prayed I felt relieved of any problems. I felt a feeling of happiness and joy. After the demons were cast out, I felt exhausted for the first two or three minutes. Then I felt like a big weight was lifted.

#9: Joseph Deragio
Birth Date: April 27, 1960
Occupation: Truck Driver
Experience: **Healed of gout**
Date of Testimony: February 8, 1999

Before I met Master Kim, I was a very mixed-up and confused individual. I was in and out of trouble with myself and my marriage. I wasn't responsible and I wasn't respectful to my wife. I would sneak off with my friends and get high and drunk. My wife didn't like this part of me, and neither did I, but I didn't know how to stop.

One day I just got so fed up with what I was doing that I decided to go look for help. I walked past the Blue Dragon Tae Kwon Do School and saw Master Kim sitting at his desk through the window. He caught my attention. I was very scared when I walked through the door and met him for the first time. Master Kim asked what I thought he and the school could do for me. I told him I needed help with my life and personal well-being. Not only did I need help with my life, but I also had a very painful medical condition called gout. It is a condition of arthritis where my joints in my body would swell up larger than normal. I was not able to walk. This would last from one to three days at each attack. There were days I would come to school in pain and Master Kim would see this. He told me he could help me with this problem. He would pray for me by laying his hands on me, and through the grace of God, would cast out the demons in me that were causing my grief. I was very skeptical about this in the beginning because I didn't believe as strongly in the Lord as I should have. Well, I am living proof that the Lord is with us. If you just reach out to God and believe in Him, there is help for you. I haven't had a gout attack in eight years. I learned how to believe and to become a better person and leave all my sadness behind. I drive a tractor-trailer to all parts of the country. During that time on the road, I never let the Bible teaching that I learned leave my heart or soul.

#10: James Caspen
Birth Date: December 20, 1968
Occupation: Carpenter
Experience: **Healed of problems with neck, ankle, back and eyes**
Date of Testimony: April 2, 1995

Before getting to know God, my life was filled with many agonizing pains. In only a few short months, my life has changed for the better. My body had been experiencing neck, ankle, back, and eye problems for many years. Master Kim has opened my eyes spiritually to get help better than expensive doctor bills. One thing I have learned is God is always loving, while the devil is always trying to destroy my life. Before taking Tae Kwon Do, I was never aware why I was plagued with so many illnesses. Through the power of Jesus Christ, Master Kim was able to cast the demons out of my body. I felt an experience I never felt before. My body experienced shakes and my eyes wanted to close when Master Kim looked in them. After he was done praying, my body felt cleansed and pain free. Master Kim has also introduced me to the Bible, and it explains the ways Jesus cast out demons for healing. Through prayer from Master Kim and myself I now feel the presence of God in my life. No matter how much you may think you have in your life, without God, you have nothing. Every day I am feeling physically and spiritually healthier. I am thankful my eyes have been opened. I am also thankful to God for never abandoning me through good and bad times.

#11: James Caspen
Birth Date: December 20, 1968
Occupation: Carpenter
Experience: **Three demons cast out**
Date of Testimony: April 6, 1995

I have been exposed to a new world, which very few under-stand. It is simply healing through God and the casting out of demons. Master Kim prayed and summoned a demon out. I truly felt the demon inside of me, and he talked through my mouth. I heard the voice inside of me, which said he's been with me for six years. He said he was sad because Jesus Christ commanded him to leave. After we prayed, I felt like the demon was truly gone, he was just one of three that have been with me for years. As of now, I am demon free, and my ankle feels great and so do all my other ailments. I have a feeling of free-dom in my body and soul. My advice to any readers would be to learn God's ways before it is too late.

#12: Michael Pyrich
Birth Date: July 15, 1953
Occupation: Digital imaging manager
Experience: **Healed of exercising injury**
Date of Testimony: October 9, 1998

I was lost and I prayed for guidance and direction in my life. Little did I know when I came to Master Kim that he would help me in ways I never expected. I trained hard and was physically better, but still I prayed for the faith and direction that I lacked. Then I had my first counseling with Master Kim. He helped me on my way, but I did not feel anything strong. When I hurt myself during my last belt test, I thought my days of training were over. Since I worked so hard to get this far, I was very depressed. Master Kim then came to me again and counseled me in the Lord. This time I allowed myself to accept Jesus Christ as my Savior and I immediately felt a veil being lifted off my body and mind. Although, I was not immediately cured of my pain, it subsided rapidly. Within two classes I was able to take one of the toughest classes since I started. I strongly believe that I came to Master Kim for a reason. As I pray for guidance every day, my faith increases. God does answer my questions and prayers.

#13: Lynn Figliano
Birth Date: January 11, 1968
Occupation: Customer Service Representative
Experience: **Healed of back pain and carpal tunnel**
Date of Testimony: April 22, 1999

A little less than a month ago, I came to see Master Kim for the first time, and it has changed my life quite a bit. I had been sick for over a year. Back pain and carpal tunnel syndrome kept me from work, and from life in every sense of the word. Those things led to surgery, physical therapies, and a great big depression. I simply did not have it in me to get myself out of my own suffering. The pain was unbearable and 1500 mg. of medication three times a day was not helping any longer. After praying with Master Kim, I felt connected to God and the pain was gone. I wake up every morning feeling good about everything, and that is a very good feeling. I have no more pain.

If the pain comes back, it would not keep me from living. I just know that God will give me whatever it takes to live my life to its fullest. No matter what had been tormenting me, I now have the knowledge to fight it. I am going back to work full time in 30 days. I truly feel blessed, and accept God in my life today and always.

#14: Ralph Collins
Birth Date: October 16, 1946
Occupation: Self-Employed
Experience: **Healed of a damaged knee that he couldn't walk on**
Date of Testimony: July 8, 1996

In March of 1966, I was drafted into the US Army. Approximately three months later during training, a piece of bone from my knee broke off. It wedged between my knee joints so the army had to operate and remove it. While they had my knee open, they also removed my cartilage. Since then, my knee kept giving me problems. With every passing year it got worse until 1995 when I was hardly able to walk on it anymore. I had to go to the VA (Veterans Administration) for help. After a lot of X-rays and bone scan X-rays, I was informed that I would be permanently disabled, and would never walk without a crutch.

I had a problem with my daughter in school. She was getting beat up and wouldn't fight back. I brought her to Master Kim so she could learn how to defend herself. When we walked in, Master Kim saw me limping and in a lot of pain. He told me that He could help me get rid of the pain. So four weeks later, Master Kim asked me to come in on a Saturday morning and I did. Master Kim explained to me about the demons that were causing my pain and that through the power of Jesus, he could get rid of them. So Master Kim prayed for me, and after a while the demons left my body. For the first time in about five years, I was able to walk up the stairs without holding on to the railing. I walked around the room for about 10 minutes without any pain. Now thanks to God, I can walk like a normal person again. God bless anyone who reads this note. Believe in God, all things are possible.

#15: Ryan Greene
Birth Date: September 19, 1971
Occupation: Project Manager/Web Designer
Experience: **Healed of allergies**
Date of Testimony: July 20, 1999

For the past two years, my allergies had been getting worse and worse. Finally I went to my doctor and he had given me two prescriptions for medication. The first muddled my thoughts, and the second gave me both terrible headaches and a terrible thirst. I came in to see Master Kim to let him know that I would be returning to class that week, as the medication had stopped me from going. He suggested that we sit down and pray together. We agreed to meet later that day. When I arrived, we went over many passages from the New Testament in the Bible that covered the casting out of demons, and how we as followers of Christ, are able to do the same.

Master Kim explained to me how he was going to pray over me. We both stood and Master Kim placed his hands on my head and started to pray. As he did, I felt most of the tension go out of my body. Soon I was relaxed and Master Kim told me to lie down. I found myself to be very tired but mentally energized at the same time. After a little while, I sat up and discussed with Master Kim what had happened and how I felt.

Master Kim emphasized two things: (1) This was not his doing, but God acting through us as an expression of our faith. (2) The important thing in life is having a close relationship with God to prevent this from happening in the future.

I have since had no problems with allergies at all. I can only attribute this to the events of this day, as no other actions have been taken.

———————

#16: Fred Marshall
Birth Date: December 29, 1965
Occupation: Restaurant Manager
Experience: **Healed from knee injury**
Date of Testimony: April 2, 1999

I always believed in a Savior that would help me in some way with my injuries—a Savior that would help me spiritually. All my life I've encountered difficulties in controlling my weight. I have also gotten injured severely resulting in broken bones, cuts, bruises, torn ligaments, tendons, etc. My temper and behavior fluctuated daily sometimes in evil sarcastic moods and sometimes good, merciful ones. It wasn't easy! For the past few years everything has gotten a lot better, but my knee would not heal. My right knee was injured a couple of years ago during a sparring session. The pain was constant during workouts and daily routines, like walking. Two months ago, I had the opportunity to meet a Grand Master of Tae Kwon Do and a relationship was formed. While talking to him about my problem, I asked him to help me. Master Kim asked me to be open-minded and invited me to come in that very same day. When I came back that evening, I was introduced to Steve who was asked to stay and pray with us. Master Kim explained to me a lot about heaven and hell, good and evil, material life, and spiritual life. We also spoke about Jesus who died and suffered to save us. We talked for an hour and we prayed. The room felt cold and I felt trapped. We started to pray asking for forgiveness of sins, and asking for strength. Master Kim made me stand up, and he put his hands on my forehead. He looked into my eyes and prayed to cast the demons out of me. My first thought was to laugh and leave, but something held me back. After a minute, a warm feeling filled me and I felt lighter and lighter after every word. He had me lie down and prayed some more. At the end, he asked me how I felt, and I told him...lightheaded! I worked out a few more days and the pain was gone. The second time I was there I told him that I was angry at everything and everybody. I also told him that I was arguing with my kids more than necessary and had no patience. We started to pray again, and I felt like pushing Master Kim away from me. Also when he was praying I felt like leaving again. Something held me back, and the same warm feeling from before entered my body, and I felt at ease with everything. He laid me down and believe me, I could have stayed there for hours. Somehow I felt secure.

I worked out a few more days and injured the tendons of my right foot. I went back to Master Kim and prayed. This time I felt warm but weak. During the prayer, I almost fell down to my knees twice, and when Master Kim laid me down, I felt something lifting my leg and I kicked. Since that day, I haven't had any problems. Sometimes the evil tries to get me again, but I pray to God and Jesus Christ, and the pain goes away. God has healed me! I'm glad I found God and Jesus Christ our Savior.

#17: Fred Marshall
Birth Date: December 29, 1965
Occupation: Restaurant Manager
Experience: **Healed of two large lumps in his body**
Date of Testimony: April 10, 2000

In December 1999, I found two small lumps on my legs. One was on my left calf, and one was on my inner thigh. Both lumps were very small, maybe about one-half inch in diameter. During three and a half months, they grew to about five and one-half inches in diameter. They had a red color and were always very hot and hurt to touch. I was very uncomfortable to do anything. The one on my left calf also caused my leg to swell up a lot, to the point that I could not walk. For three months I went to three different doctors and they had me go to 12 different tests, including a biopsy with the suspicion of a tumor. Nothing was found and the lumps continued to grow even more. Not having treatment or antibiotics for more than three months made it worse. Finally, I decided to talk to Grand Master Kim one more time. He showed me in 1998 all the benefits of faith and prayer. He once again spoke to me about Jesus Christ and His power against evil spirits, demons, and all other sources of negative power and energy that wants to bring us down all the time. We prayed. He prayed over me looking straight in my eyes. He helped me to understand the healing powers of God through Jesus Christ and our faith. He cast the demons out.

Then I got better. I am living proof of it. Today, two weeks after the praying session with Grand Master Kim, I have no more bumps. I have no more pain. My legs are no longer swollen, and I am new and back on track. I am back in the gym and my life is back in order. My body is a clean house with no room for demons. Thank you God for giving your strength and light back into my life.

#18: Hal Iratel
Birth Date: September 25, 1962
Occupation: Data Manager
Experience: **Healed of a hand injury**
Date of Testimony: June 8, 1999

While at practice one evening, I received an injury to my right hand. I was hesitant to tell Master Kim, then I decided to. So I showed Master Kim my hand. He started to massage it, and then we decided to pray about it. I am a religious person but haven't been going to church lately. So we started to pray. Master Kim laid his hand upon my head as we prayed. While praying, I felt this energy come up from my stomach to my head as if it was flowing out of my body. We spent a good half-hour praying. After the prayer, I felt like a big stone was lifted off my back. I felt so relaxed that I was tired. We spoke a while longer. That same night I went to sleep peacefully. I now have a sense of awareness. I worry less and my hand feels better. At first I was skeptical, but where there is faith there is God. One must also realize that temptation comes in many different forms, and that evil never sleeps. Amen.

#19: Ulf Lilienthal
Birth Date: September 23, 1961
Occupation: Sales Rep
Experience: **Healed of a headache, foot injury, and the common cold**
Date of Testimony: September 23, 1999

I sit here on my 38th birthday writing what many may think is an unbelievable story. A little over a year ago, a good friend of mine and colleague at work approached me about meeting over lunch to discuss Jesus Christ. Being a good Christian, or so I thought, I agreed immediately. I have to admit that I was a bit nervous about what Steve's approach would be. To my delight, Steve turned out to be a genuine worker for Christ. In Steve's explanation to me about the battle between good and evil and the origin of disease, he told me his personal story and about his Tae Kwon Do Grand Master, Master Kim. He also told me how Master Kim helped him find God's strength to beat cancer. While I believed this wholeheartedly, and since that day I have been a passionate soldier for God, I really longed to experience firsthand the encounter between good and evil and God's grace. Steve cast out a demon from me the day we met, but other than a slight headache going away, I hadn't really experienced the feeling of peace I wanted. My children were starting to take Tae Kwon Do lessons, and I decided I would join as well. I signed up for classes in August and began meeting with Master Kim. The next day I felt terrible. I had a bad cold and a very bad pain in my right foot. I had it for about two weeks prior. It started shortly after I began training, but I thought it was normal aches and pains. I realized what was going on so I prayed hard and tried to cast out the demons myself, but I would get exhausted. The pain would ease temporarily but would come back just as strong. I was finally able to go to Tae Kwon Do class again on Saturday 9/18, (there was a hurricane in between) and I tried to train, but my foot still hurt badly. Master Kim knew about it and asked how I was doing. When I told him, he said we should pray. He prayed for me and cast out the demons. He was very intense and I could feel God's power. When I got up to leave, my foot was already beginning to get better. By that evening the pain was completely gone. By the next day, my cold was even going away. I have had no problem with the foot ever since, and I have trained three times on it, twice very hard with lots of jumping and kicking.

This experience helped met to see how serious the fight between good and evil is, and how deep our faith needs to be to win the battle. I look forward to working with Master Kim and Steve to not only further my learning of Tae Kwon Do, but more importantly to grow in fellowship with them as brothers in Christ's army.

#20: Marvin Boyston
Birth Date: November 4, 1954
Occupation: Teacher
Experience: **Healed of enlarged heart and a bone spur on his heel**
Date of Testimony: April 2, 1998

On April 6, 1997, I had a heart attack. I was dead and revived five minutes later. Two months later, my Tae Kwon Do School closed down and I needed to rehabilitate myself. I thought only of physical rehabilitation. When I met Master Kim, he and I both knew that this was the new school for me. He said he would help me mentally, physically, and spiritually. When I started at this school, Master Kim noticed I had problems with my left heel. I had a bone spur on the bottom of my heel. Every time I stepped, it would give me tremendous pain. A doctor advised either total rest or surgery that would leave me on crutches for months. When I explained this to Master Kim, he sat me down and showed me about getting back in touch with Jesus. I went to Catholic grammar school, high school, and college, but had drifted away from church. One Saturday morning, Master Kim and I read scriptures from the Bible and prayed. He prayed with me and over me, and asked Jesus to help me rid myself of Satan. It felt good to be praying again and thanking Jesus. Within a few days, my two-year-old problem disappeared. There can be no other explanation than my prayer to God. I had been away too long. And my heart attack? I have had two stress tests and three electrocardiograms in the past year. On one of them, a nurse (who did not know my heart attack story), wanted to know why I was having my heart checked. When I told her that I had a heart attack and was no longer breathing, she was incredulous. She could find no scar tissue or damage that is always easily seen during one of these tests. My heart shows no sign of a life-ending heart attack. (After the heart attack I was in the hospital recovering for one week and out of work for two months.) Feel my heel, listen to my heart, and pray.

#21: Robin Parker
Birth Date: February 13, 1954
Occupation: Real Estate
Experience: **Healed from optic neuritis (vision restored)**
Date of Testimony: December 1, 1998

My problems started in September 1998. I was going through a tough time with my marriage. From all the stress, I developed optic-neuritis, which affected me rapidly. My eye in one week lost 40 percent vision, and the second week I lost 80 percent. I had every test there was and the ophthalmologist said it could be related to MS. He sent me to a neurologist and for an MRI. All crazy things went through my head about how I would function as a single mom, take my son to school, plus go to work and support us if I lost my vision. But the answer was there all the time. I was too clouded in my mind to realize that I had Jesus Christ with me every minute and hour of my day. I remembered how He heard me before and helped me through migraine headaches and my son through anxiety problems. So I started to close my mind to the negative and open it to the positive. I prayed and talked to God and also read the Bible. He heard me and I felt comforted. Gradually my vision started to return. I asked Master Kim to pray with me because he is a strong Christian. He has taught me how to pray and be thankful to the Lord. Two months later my eye is almost normal after being told I could have remained blind in one eye. Life is still a struggle, but just having my son and me in good health means more than anything else. My son never lets me forget that the Lord has helped us and to never miss church. For me as a single mom being reassured from my 11-year-old son that God is always there for us is a blessing in itself.

#22: Joseph Carepo
Birth Date: May 23, 1977
Occupation: Student
Experience: **Healed of a knee injury and stomach virus**
Date of Testimony: April 14, 1999

About two weeks ago, I went to a Wednesday night Tae Kwon Do class. We did the same routine exercises that we've always been doing. The day after, I woke up experiencing a tremendous pain in my left knee. It was painful to the point that I could barely walk. So right away, I consulted Master Kim. We made an appointment on the Saturday morning of the same week my injury had occurred. Master Kim asked me why my knee started hurting and my response was none other than "I don't know." Then Master Kim had me read testimonies, similar to the one I'm writing right now. I couldn't believe what I was reading! To tell you the truth, I wasn't a very religious person to begin with. Inevitably my response to these testimonies was rather skeptical. Master Kim proceeded to explain the purpose of the Bible and the concept of good and bad. After doing this, he prayed for me. In the midst of this whole praying session, tears began to roll down my face and there was a feeling of resistance. I felt great relief and voila! My knee was in fact better. After this whole experience, I look at the world from a totally different perspective. But the demon was determined to do his dirty job, despite his expulsion from my body. A few days later, I became sick and was diagnosed with a stomach virus. I threw up excessively to the point that I lost ten pounds. I tried eating to maintain a regular diet, but I would throw it all up in a matter of minutes. Also, one night during this week, I had been experiencing insomnia until 6:00 AM. I went to visit Master Kim and he prayed for me again, casting out the demon that kept insisting on bothering me. Through prayers and God's mercy, I felt a great release of tension. Now my knee injury is completely gone (with no medical remedies)! I can honestly say that things are certainly looking up for me. More importantly, however, is the feeling of comfort that God is next to me all the time.

#23: Paul Arista
Birth Date: November 22, 1972
Occupation: Teacher
Experience: **Healed of ankle pain and a bad sore throat**
Date of Testimony: February 20, 1995

I have been training with Master Kim the past three years and getting closer to God. About two years ago, I injured my left ankle while training. I thought I would be able to treat it myself but the pain persisted for about two weeks. Master Kim finally took me to the side on Saturday afternoon and explained to me the healing powers of God. The devil is always out to get us and take us away from God. He sends his minions to bring us disease, misery, and pain. Now, I was raised Catholic and still practice my faith but I never realized that my faith and God's power could heal me. I guess I never really took much consideration in the stories of Jesus healing those who believed in God's power. I was, in a sense, like the blind man. Now my eyes are open. Master Kim laid his hands on me and cast out a demon who was sent to pull me away from my Lord. It was the most powerful spiritual experience in my life, and when all was said and done, a great sense of peace came over me. The ankle pain was gone and has never returned. My health has improved. Since then, I had a really bad sore throat, and it was so severe that I couldn't breathe. I was healed through the power of God. I even felt the demon leave as my throat cleared. My faith in my Savior cured me again, and probably saved my life. I assure you this is not a ploy to join a church or a hoax. The events I described above have brought me closer to God reaffirming my faith. Now I live at peace with myself, others, and the Lord. Your faith in God will cure you, and it is more practical and reliable than any healthcare practice.

#24: Jack Ward
Birth Date: April 6, 1971
Occupation: Physical Therapist
Experience: **Healed of gastric intestinal problems, allergies,
      & a knee injury**
Date of Testimony: June 6, 1997

As a professional in the health care field, I encounter many problems, whether they be physical or mental. I myself have been subject to many mishaps and the testimony that I'm giving today is to document my experience with the healing power of the Lord our Savior Jesus.

The first time that I was healed was about 12 years ago. I was 14 at the time, and a student of Master Kim. I had months of gastrointestinal problems in which I had a lot of pain. One day during class, the pain was so severe that I was unable to stand up. Master Kim at that time took me aside and began to pray over me. At first I did not know what to think, but as he went on, I began to feel very weak. The pain became worse and my stomach was burning. I began to feel hot and started to sweat. The room started to spin, and the next thing I knew was that I was lying on the floor with Master Kim still praying over me. The pain had decreased and each day improved. Until this day, I have not experienced that kind of pain again.

I was too young to understand what had happened. A few months ago, I had injured my left knee. It was the type of pain that I knew was serious, and that may take a long time to heal. Nevertheless, Master Kim took me aside and explained to me that Jesus died for our sins so that we may be forgiven. He also explained that evil spirits are the cause of our injuries and problems. Master Kim prayed over me and cast out the spirits that were causing my pain. Within a matter of a few weeks, my injury was completely healed when it should have taken a few months. My last experience was about two months ago. I have had allergies for the past two years. I had the typical signs such as red eyes, runny nose, sneezing, congestion, and difficulties breathing. Again Master Kim cast out the spirits causing my ailments. My allergies were gone, and all symptoms disappeared. I felt so much better. This all occurred during the worst time of the year for allergies. I am a true believer, and have accepted the Holy Spirit and God into my life. I hope that my experiences will one day benefit others so that they too may be healed and live a better life.

---

25 Tom Havenerra
Birth Date: August 15, 1969
Occupation: Teacher
Experience: **Healed of migraines**
Date of Testimony: December 8, 2000

Since the age of 12, I've experienced serious headaches three or four times each week. Like both of my parents, I was diagnosed with migraine headaches, and accepted the idea that I'd have to live with the pain for the rest of my life. In the past six months, the headaches have gotten more and more serious, and equally hard to deal with. During the month of September 2000, I experienced headaches daily. They became so severe, I was often unable to eat, stand, or sleep. I began a routine of coming home from work feeling bad, and ending up suffering in bed for the remainder of the day.

Thank God I enrolled in Master Kim's Blue Dragon Tae Kwon Do Academy in October of 2000. After several weeks of preparation, Master Kim arranged for us to meet so he could teach me to eliminate the suffering. We scheduled to meet on November 11, and I was forced to cancel, due to a death in the family. We rescheduled to meet on November 15, and I was again forced to cancel due to another death in the family. Another appointment was made for November 18, and Master Kim had to cancel. It seemed as if some force was attempting to keep me from the knowledge Master Kim was offering to share.

We met on November 22 and the lesson began. Master Kim, another student and I read several scriptures from the New Testament. I came to understand that the cause of my trouble was evil spirits. We prayed together and Master Kim put his hands on my head and commanded the demon to leave my body in the name of Jesus Christ. My body began to convulse as Master Kim cast out the demon. After some more prayer, I felt renewed, the pain was gone, and a wonderful feeling permeated my body. Glory to God.

#26: Charles Hannett
Birth Date: November 29, 1945
Occupation: Former VP of Sales
Experience: **Healed from some stroke damage**
Date of Testimony: May 17, 1995

I am happy to write down the story I have related to others many times. In the fall of 1991, I suffered a serious stroke. The area damaged affected all motor functions. After spending nine days in intensive care, the doctors weren't sure if I'd live, or ever leave a wheelchair. The following eight months were spent in therapy at the Kessler Institute for Rehabilitation. I was discharged June 17, 1992. My balance was poor, and I was barely able to walk, except for the use of a cane.

On May 28, 1994, I met a Master in Tae Kwon Do, Dong Jin Kim. Until that day, I needed a cane to go everywhere. As a practicing Catholic, I saw no harm in meeting with a Christian man who offered to help me. There were no strings and no charge. He just wanted to help me. During our meeting, he gave me new insight into the spiritual world. He prayed over me, casting out demons. This was all very strange, and new to me. But the moment he finished praying, I commented on a trickle of sweat that ran down my chest. He felt there, it was dry. After thanking him he said: "Don't thank me, thank God." As I got up to leave, my weak foot felt lighter, unlike before. Instinctively I reached for my cane. "If you take that cane now," he said, "you'll never get rid of it."

My wife was waiting in the car since she had come to take me home. It was then that I "carried" a new cane, barely two weeks old, outside and placed it in the gutter. As she drove home I tried to explain everything. It was just too much. I was overwhelmed. Saturday, May 28, "I walked" to and from the five o'clock Mass at St. Mary's Church in Rutherford without a cane! It felt strange. I couldn't stop crying, I was so happy. Positive suggestion? Read on.

After being impotent since the stroke, my potency returned two days later. One week later my blood pressure plummeted. I called my doctor. He reduced my medication more that half. Now a year later, I still continue to improve. I still have a long way to go, but I keep improving. In April, I had a follow-up sonogram to check a blockage in my neck found last year. My doctor said it was calcified and corrected by surgery. This April the pathologist told me it was reduced by 10 percent. From May last year, my life has changed, and my faith strengthened. Now when I read the Bible (a rarity before), the words have true meaning, they have substance. As strange and unorthodox as all this sounds, how can I hesitate to doubt the words: "Where two or three are gathered in My name, I am there."

#27: Barbara Elzahy
Birth Date: June 29, 1959
Occupation: Technical Assistant
Experience: **Healed of breast cancer**
Date of Testimony: March 23, 2002

The problem that God healed me from was breast cancer. My cancer was discovered when I went for a mammogram in January 23, 2001, and it showed abnormality in my left breast. At the time, the doctor recommended surgery and the removal of the lump in my breast. After the surgery, the doctors told me that I had breast cancer in stage 1, and the size of my tumor was two centimeters. The doctors told me that I needed another surgery and node sampling to evaluate my condition. I went for surgery on March 28, 2001 and the doctors told me there was still a problem and that they recommended chemotherapy. I refused that idea. I only went for one treatment and that was radiation.

In the mean time, I was desperate and going crazy. When I came to Master Kim and told him about my problem, Master Kim told me that I wouldn't have any problem if I listened to Jesus Christ. He explained that my disease was caused by demons, and he showed me the way to cast them out from my body. Consequently, I can say today that God has cured me.

#28: Jennie Hernandez
Birth Date: August 8, 1971
Occupation: Sales Associate
Experience: **Toddler healed from seizures**
Date of Testimony: February 16, 2002

On February 16, 2002, our 18-month-old son, Shane Matthew, awoke in the early morning with a fever. All week he had been fighting a cold. We gave him Tylenol & rocked him back to sleep. Around 7 A.M., he awoke again. The fever was 101.3 and he was very cranky. I had a very strong feeling that I should take him to the doctor. While we were in the waiting room, Shane did not even move. The doctor started the examination. She turned her back for a moment to get something. Shane was in my arms and then started to shake. I screamed, "DOCTOR, WHAT IS HAPPENING TO MY BABY?" She told me that he was having a seizure. The doctor ripped Shane's clothes off and proceeded to carry him to a large sink. She was patting him down with cold water. He continued to have the seizure. The doctor took him to a table, then he started to turn blue. His little body was becoming lifeless. The doctor was giving him oxygen. I started crying out to God, "LORD, PLEASE DON'T LET MY BABY DIE!"

I called my husband. I told him that Shane had a seizure. He could not believe what I was saying. I also told him to call Katie & Steve (my sister & brother-in-law). They really know God. I went back into the room with baby Shane. He was screaming his head off. The ambulance had finally gotten to the doctor's office. He screamed the entire ambulance ride. One of the EMTs told me the screaming was music to her ears. This is because screaming meant that he was still conscious. Her comment made me feel a little better, but I was still scared.

At the hospital, Shane was still screaming. His temperature was now 104.9. His eyes were all bloodshot. His arms were fixed in a stretched-out position and his hands were bent back. My husband and brother-in-law arrived at the hospital. My husband was very concerned that our son was going to have permanent brain damage when he saw Shane's condition. An intern examined him and told us that he had a very sore throat. At this point I knew that I had to put all my faith in God.

I left my son with my husband, and went to pray with my brother-in-law. He prayed for my son and me very intensely. He shared Isaiah 53:5, "And by His stripes we are healed." We prayed for the evil bothering my son to leave in the name of Jesus Christ. It did! When we came back, my son was drinking a bottle with his dad. His hands and arms went back to normal. Finally the doctor examined him. The doctor told us that he would be fine, that his fever was practically gone, and that the baby didn't even have a sore throat anymore! God healed Shane completely. THANK YOU, LORD!

Chapter XIV
Time to Break Free!

It is now time for **you** to break free from the devil. It is time for **you** to stand strong in the power and the might of Jesus Christ. You have read God's promises from His word, and have heard from dozens of people who have already been healed. Now is **your** time! It is time to break free from all oppression of the devil. It is time to break free from all of your pain, trouble, sickness, weakness, and everything that is evil.

Whatever your trouble, no matter how bad, how long you have been suffering, how much damage has been done, nothing is impossible for God Almighty. God is going to heal you through the power of His Son, Jesus Christ. The enemy cannot stop you from getting blessing if you truly believe the Father's promise!

If you haven't made the decision to trust Jesus Christ as your personal Savior, you must take this first step. Submit to God, and believe that the Lord Jesus Christ is the only begotten Son of God who died for your sins. Do not hold back. This is the biggest decision in your entire life because this decision determines where you will be spending the rest of eternity! If you miss your chance to make a decision to follow Christ, all is lost!

Tell Jesus right now that you accept Him as Lord of your life, that you believe in Him, that you want to receive the Holy Spirit, and that you will turn away from your sin. The Bible says,

> Therefore, as the Holy Spirit says: "Today, if you will hear
> His voice, Do not harden your hearts..." (Hebrews 3:7–8)

Put your fears and inhibitions aside, and let Jesus Christ make you His child. The devil knows he is defeated if you accept Jesus Christ as your personal Savior. Don't let him block you from accepting God's grace.

> Humble yourselves in the sight of the Lord, and He will
> lift you up. (James 4:10)

> ...that if you confess with your mouth the Lord Jesus and
> believe in your heart that God has raised Him from the
> dead, you will be saved. For with the heart one believes
> unto righteousness, and with the mouth confession is made
> unto salvation. For the Scripture says, "Whoever believes
> on Him will not be put to shame." (Romans 10:9–11)

Desire God's grace with all of your heart, mind, and soul and you will receive it! You can pray this prayer (as a guide), telling Jesus you accept Him into your heart.

> Jesus, I realize I am a sinner and need to be forgiven of
> my sins. I no longer want to live my life separated from
> You. I believe that You are the Son of God, and that You
> died so that I can be forgiven of my sins. I accept You as
> my personal Savior and turn away from my sin. I want
> to go forward trusting You as the Lord of my life, and
> will follow You all my days. Please save me, and send
> Your Holy Spirit to me! I ask this in the name of Jesus
> Christ. Amen.

AMEN! Praying this from your heart means that you are now saved, and an heir to the Kingdom of God! You have now been forgiven of your sin and are no longer slave to the devil! You are free! You are now able to receive the many blessings God has prepared for you. You now have power and authority over the devil. It's time to take action!

> "Until now you have asked nothing in My name. Ask, and
> you will receive, that your joy may be full." (John 16:24)

God's Instruction on How to Cast Out an Evil Spirit

Read this next section very closely so you can pray for yourself, and cast out your sickness or problem in the name of Jesus Christ. Sit down in a quiet place and take a couple of deep breaths and relax. All you have to do is act on God's word, and He will follow through with His promise that

"...by His stripes we are healed." (Isaiah 53:5)

STEP 1:

Tell your enemy aloud that you are a child of Jesus Christ. Tell Satan that he no longer controls you, and that Jesus Christ is going to heal you today. It may feel strange to speak aloud, but the Bible repeatedly demonstrates that we should speak God's word. Tell Satan that you are a free and redeemed child of Jesus, and that by the stripes of Jesus Christ you are healed!

STEP 2:

Stand strong in the position that Jesus has prepared for you. Command the sickness to get out of your body. Command it in the name of Jesus Christ to leave. Jesus repeatedly demonstrated this, and we are now called to follow his example. (Mark 16:17) Specifically say,

"I COMMAND YOU TO LEAVE ME IN THE NAME OF JESUS CHRIST!"

This is not magic or an incantation. This is you, a child of God, ordering evil out of your body by the power of Jesus' name. Repeat this command until you know that you have believed. Whether you need to pray for one minute or one hour is inconsequential. Just persevere until you are sure you have received God's blessing. Ask Jesus to help you, and He will guide you.

The devil will attempt to resist, but it doesn't matter. He will send many thoughts and feelings to distract you, but keep your faith and focus fixed on the promise of God through Jesus Christ. No sickness can stay in your body in front of the name of Jesus Christ. It's God's spiritual law. We are always made victorious in the name of Jesus Christ.

Although you may feel something in your body, know that signs are unimportant. Do not look for signs. Trust in the word of God only. Remember that God is faithful. It is His promise that you are healed. You just need to believe in His promise. Pray until you have overcome. Give one final command for the sickness to never return!

"LEAVE ME IN THE NAME OF JESUS CHRIST, AND NEVER RETURN!"

This prayer in faith means that you are healed! Thank and praise God for healing you!

STEP 3:

Act on your faith. If you couldn't walk, begin walking. If you couldn't see well, pick up something and read it. This is not to test God, but this is to act on what you already believe. If you fully believe in the promise of Jesus Christ when you prayed, your problem has left and you are healed. God is faithful always. Don't worry if your problem doesn't feel like it left immediately, just trust God and blessing will follow. Continue to praise and give thanks to Him.

STEP 4:

Tell people how God has blessed you! Write down on a piece of paper what God has done for you along with your thanks and praise to Him. Telling people about the blessing you have received greatly pleases God. Send us your story by visiting our web site at www.conquerorsinchrist.org. We would love to hear what God has done in your life.

STEP 5:

Now to protect yourself, do your best to *"...not walk according to the flesh but according to the spirit."* (Romans 8:4) Do your best not to sin. Remember Jesus' words...

> **"When an unclean spirit goes out of a man, he goes through dry places, seeking rest, and finds none. Then he says, 'I will return to my house from which I came.' And when he comes, he finds it empty, swept, and put in order. Then he goes and takes with him seven other spirits more wicked than himself, and they enter and dwell there; and the last**

state of that man is worse than the first. So shall it also be with this wicked generation." (Matthew 12:43–45)

Look straight ahead and don't doubt the work that Jesus Christ has done for you. Don't look back. You have received an awesome blessing from God. Live an abundant life in the freedom of Christ. Amen!

We want to hear about the great things God has done for you! Visit Conquerors In Christ World Ministries at www.conquerorsinchrist.org. We are available to pray with you, and look forward to answering any questions you may have. Please review the next chapter to better understand what your future holds.

Chapter XV
What Your Future Holds

The Christian struggle against evil is waged continually day and night until we go to heaven. The devil and his army work 24 hours a day attempting to kill, steal, and destroy in every and any way they can. Rather than cause for alarm, this should serve as a strong call to action. We must equip ourselves in the spirit daily being ready and watchful, always growing stronger in the grace and knowledge of Jesus Christ. We must have an attitude which gives thanks to God in all situations, and we must use every adversity as an opportunity to train and grow stronger in the spirit. When things get difficult, don't get discouraged. The Bible says that we should expect attack from Satan, and not to doubt our position as beloved children of Jesus Christ.

> **Beloved, do not think it strange concerning the fiery trial which is to try you, as though some strange thing happened to you;... (1 Peter 4:12)**

You are now a soldier for the Kingdom of God. Leave your former way of life and live in the holiness that is only possible with Jesus Christ.

> **The night is far spent, the day is at hand. Therefore let us cast off the works of darkness, and let us put on the armor of light. Let us walk properly, as in the day, not in revelry**

and drunkenness, not in lewdness and lust, not in strife and envy. But put on the Lord Jesus Christ, and make no provision for the flesh, to fulfill its lusts. (Romans 13:12–14)

You therefore must endure hardship as a good soldier of Jesus Christ. No one engaged in warfare entangles himself with the affairs of this life, that he may please him who enlisted him as a soldier. (2 Timothy 2:3–4)

This kind of life isn't easy, and most choose not to live it, but if you endure, Jesus Christ's strength will sustain and keep you. You will truly become a conqueror in Christ. Do not worry about your life, or anything in it for that matter. Obey God at all times and you will fully understand this verse.

Who shall separate us from the love of Christ? Shall tribulation, or distress, or persecution, or famine, or nakedness, or peril, or sword? As it is written: "For Your sake we are killed all day long; We are accounted as sheep for the slaughter." Yet in all these things we are more than conquerors through Him who loved us. For I am persuaded that neither death nor life, nor angels nor principalities nor powers, nor things present nor things to come, nor height nor depth, nor any other created thing, shall be able to separate us from the love of God which is in Christ Jesus our Lord. (Romans 8:35–39)

Yes, nothing in all of creation has the power to separate you from the love of God. This means that no trial, sickness, or weakness can overcome you. The Father loves you that much. It is this understanding that will guard your heart and mind in Jesus Christ. Remember...

But the Lord is faithful, who will establish you and guard you from the evil one. (2 Thessalonians 3:3)

Make no mistake. We are called to have complete peace in the midst of struggle. The world has difficulty understanding this because its peace is dependent upon circumstances. If the day was stressful, they became stressed. If the day had problems, they had problems. If the day was depressing, they were depressed. This should not be so with a Christian. The world could be falling down around us, but because our peace is tied to Jesus Christ, and not the frailty of circumstances, our peace is unshakable. His peace is the strength of our hearts, minds, feelings, health, and very lives.

> **"Peace I leave with you, My peace I give to you; not as the world gives do I give to you. Let not your heart be troubled, neither let it be afraid." (John 14:27)**

Tell the World...

The greatest honor known to any man or women is to bring glory to Jesus Christ and be used for the work of His Kingdom. The knowledge provided in the Bible is meant to be shared and to go forth as light into a hurting world. Desire to be used by God and He will lead you in every step. Introduce people to the promises of Jesus Christ, and help to lead them to an understanding of who He is so they too may become children of God. Remember...

> **"...As the Father has sent Me, I also send you." (John 20:21)**

> **"Heal the sick, cleanse the lepers, raise the dead, cast out demons. Freely you have received, freely give." (Matthew 10:8)**

Listen to the final words of Jesus Christ before He was lifted up to Heaven. They are the instructions we should take seriously and follow.

> **And He said to them, "Go into all the world and preach the gospel to every creature. He who believes and is baptized will be saved; but he who does not believe will be condemned. And these signs will follow those who believe: In My name they will cast out demons; they will speak with new tongues; they will take up serpents; and if they drink anything deadly, it will by no means hurt them; they will lay hands on the sick, and they will recover." (Mark 16:15–18)**

> **And Jesus came and spoke to them, saying, "All authority has been given to Me in heaven and on earth. Go therefore**

and make disciples of all the nations, baptizing them in the name of the Father and of the Son and of the Holy Spirit, teaching them to observe all things that I have commanded you; and lo, I am with you always, even to the end of the age. Amen." (Matthew 28:18–20)

Conclusion

It is truly time to praise God for all that He has done for you. It is time to give Him all the glory and honor in your life. Never stop learning and growing. Read the Bible daily, and find a good church which follows and teaches the doctrine of the Bible. Keep focused and stay strong.

"This Book of the Law shall not depart from your mouth, but you shall meditate in it day and night, that you may observe to do according to all that is written in it. For then you will make your way prosperous, and then you will have good success. Have I not commanded you? Be strong and of good courage; do not be afraid, nor be dismayed, for the Lord your God is with you wherever you go." (Joshua 1:8–9)

May you live the blessed and abundant life that God the Father has provided through His Son, Jesus Christ. May you live courageously and victoriously as a true Conqueror in Christ! Amen.

Summary

1. God created the heavens and the earth. (Genesis 1:1)
2. God privileged mankind with the greatest authority in all His creation. (Genesis 1:26)
3. God commanded Adam and Eve not to eat the fruit of the tree of the knowledge of good and evil. (Genesis 2:16–17)
4. Satan tempted Adam and Eve to eat the fruit of the tree of the knowledge of good and evil, and they disobeyed God. (Genesis 3:1–6)
5. Adam and Eve lost their position of authority on earth, and Satan gained access to plague the earth with pain and destruction. (Genesis 3:14–19)
6. God sent His only begotten Son, Jesus Christ, to pay the penalty of our sin by dying on a cross, so those who believe in Him would have eternal life. (John 3:16–18)
7. Jesus Christ rose from the dead and destroyed the works of the devil restoring us back to the Father. (Ephesians 2:1–10, 1 John 3:8)
8. Jesus Christ empowered believers with the Holy Spirit. (John 14:15–18, Acts 1:8)
9. Jesus Christ gives us power and authority to overcome the enemy so that we may be healed. (Luke 10:19, Matthew 10:8)
10. Jesus Christ makes us more than conquerors through faith in His name! (Mark 16:17–18, John 14:12–14, Acts 3:16, Acts 4:10)

Keys to Overcome

- Accept God's promise to be made spiritually alive by placing your faith in His only begotten Son, Jesus Christ, so that you can break free from the power of Satan, and become a child of God. (John 3:16)
- Look past the physical world, and recognize the spiritual world is living, active, and impacts your daily life.
- Understand that your struggles take place in the spiritual realm, and not in the physical realm. (Ephesians 6)
- Understand that Satan and his army are the root to every form of destruction including sickness, disease, and tribulation.
- Stand strong in the promises of God through Jesus Christ so that you can resist and overcome the devil in the name of Jesus Christ and be victorious. We are made free from all sickness and disease by the pain and suffering Jesus Christ endured for us. (Isaiah 53:4–5)
- Protect your body and mind in Christ by avoiding sin and growing strong in the spirit through prayer and Bible study.

More Amazing Stories

#1: Peter Maki
Birth Date: May 10, 1961
Occupation: Stock Trader
Experience: **Healed of mental stress and problems with his back, neck, shoulder, and knee**
Date of Testimony: April 1, 1995

I work in a very high-pressure industry and was having difficulty dealing with it. I could not sleep, my stomach hurt, I was irritable, and basically I was a wreck. Master Kim consoled me and we knelt together and prayed together. He reminded me that if I believed in Jesus Christ (and I do) that everything else was trivial. He explained that Jesus Christ already died for my sins so whatever demons were bothering me had to leave if we confronted them with these facts. That's what we did and I immediately felt better. I was totally exhausted because I hadn't had a good night's sleep in months but it was a great feeling of relief. I went home, thanked God, and slept for 18 hours straight. When I awoke, I had never felt better. Throughout our five years of friendship we have used the power of Jesus Christ to help me dozens of times with back, neck, shoulder, knee injuries to name a few. My physical, mental, and spiritual strength has never been greater, and I thank God everyday for my well-being.

#2: Bacilio Egoavil
Birth Date: April 30, 1973
Occupation: Computer Consultant
Experience: **Helped with asthma and a back injury**
Date of Testimony: March 6, 1997

I have suffered from asthma for many years. One day I told Master Kim of my problem with asthma. To my surprise, he said he could help me. Yes, I admit I was a little bit hesitant and concerned with the idea, but I had nothing to lose. Master Kim and I sat down and talked about life. He asked me what I thought happens after death, and I told him I believe we go to heaven. He asked me the key question "Do you believe in Jesus?" Of course, I said yes. He explained to me that Jesus is the gate of heaven, and He is our Savior. Master Kim also explained to me that Jesus will always forgive us of our sins just as long as we believe. Then I started to read different scriptures from the Bible. Now I was ready. He put his hands over my head and told the demon to get out. I know this sounds a little weird but it is true. Before I knew it, tears were pouring out of my eyes, and let me tell you, I'm not one to cry. Finally it was all over. I felt so lightheaded and relaxed, it was a positive feeling.

That was my first incident. My second was when I was in the gym, and I hurt my lower back. Once again Master Kim prayed for me by casting out the demons. I was fine afterwards, but let me tell you that once you beat the demons, you must pray harder and become stronger because they will try to get back in you. That's what the Bible states, and they bring seven more. I am not 100 percent completely healed with my asthma, but I am a lot better. I would honestly say about 85 percent better. I know with time and faith I will overcome this situation completely. What I do want to say to anyone that is reading this is you must believe in Jesus. I know that some of you probably have a hard time believing in something that does not physically exist, but that's what faith is all about.

#3: Carl Figueroa
Birth Date: March 3, 1970
Occupation: Law Student
Experience: **Healed of allergies (pollen), throat problems,
    and a vision problem**
Date of Testimony: March 28, 1995

Whenever the pollen season arrived, I would become susceptible to hay fever. My eyes would get extremely irritated, my nose was always runny, and I would constantly sneeze. A very close friend of mine told me about Master Kim, and how faithful he was to God. This was in the spring of 1992 when I first decided to speak to Master Kim about the word of God in the Bible.

Master Kim witnessed to me about our Lord and Savior Jesus Christ, and the omnipotence of our heavenly Father. Master Kim showed me in scripture the way Jesus Christ cast out demons who possessed human beings. It is by the power of the Holy Spirit that children of God, like Mr. Kim, can command evil spirits to get out of our bodies, through the name of Jesus Christ! By restoring my faith in God and confessing that Jesus Christ was crucified for a wretched soul like me, my sins were forgiven. Then Mr. Kim was able to expel the illness of hay fever within me. Mr. Kim prayed over me and laid hands on me in the name of our Lord Jesus Christ for about one hour. To this day, as God is my witness, I have not been afflicted with any hay fever or similar symptoms since. Thanks be to God!

Recently, as the New Year began, I had been feeling very lightheaded, dizzy, confused, and I was unable to concentrate. The next day, when I went to school everything was blurry and hazy, almost as if a cloud was in my line of vision. Even when I put on my eyeglasses, I could not see clearly. I prayed to God and called on the name of Jesus Christ for help. That same evening, Mr. Kim and I prayed together. Mr. Kim laid hands on me and with the power of the Holy Spirit, in Christ's name, the demon was expelled from my body.

Another time, my throat was extremely sore, to the point that I was "hoarse," I could not speak loudly at all without it hurting me. I went to the hospital for medicine, but the injection they gave me did not help me. Master Kim warned me how the devil would never stop trying to keep me away from God and His righteousness. Mr. Kim again prayed over me and laid his hands on me and expelled the evil sprits from my body in the name of Jesus Christ. I had no control over my body. I fell straight back and slammed down to the ground. I give all the glory and honor to Almighty God for helping me in the name of Jesus Christ.

#4: Ted Brighton
Birth Date: April 28, 1970
Occupation: Computer Technology
Experience: **Healed from emotional problems and pain from AIDS**
Date of Testimony: February 8, 2000

One day in September of 1994, I was not feeling well. I decided to go to the doctor to get a physical checkup. While there, I decided to get a HIV test done also. A couple of days later I was called back to the office for the results. Physically I was O.K. except for the fact that I was HIV+. It hit me like a hammer. I had to tell my wife and have her tested. She was pregnant with our daughter. Also, my 3-year-old son had to be tested. The news was devastating. Luckily, my daughter was blessed by God and was born without a trace of HIV in her blood as well as my son. Unfortunately, my wife's results also came back positive. She forgave me, but never trusted me again. The next few years after that were rocky, with constant fighting over this and that. Eventually, I didn't want to live anymore. I just wanted to end it all rather than to keep on living with this horrible pain. I turned to drugs, which ruined my life even more. Our marriage got worse. Eventually we were separated. She couldn't keep on living the lie we were living. So I decided to join Master Kim's class, to try and change my life around. The exercise had me feeling pretty good about myself, but there was still something haunting me, fogging up my head, until Master Kim came to talk to me. My wife had gotten upset with me that very night and said she didn't ever want to speak to me again, which hurt me deeply. We still had a relationship, and now that was taken away from me. I was depressed and didn't know what to do. That night Master Kim introduced me to the Bible and he told me if I had faith and believed in God and the Holy Spirit, things would look a lot clearer to me. So I told Master Kim I had faith and did want to win the battle over this deadly disease, so we prayed to God. Master Kim cast out the evil spirit that was holding a fog over me. After we prayed, my shoulders felt as if a ton of bricks had been removed from them and I felt better. Since then I've been reading the Bible day and night and have gone to church. Things seem better now, thanks to God.

#5: Florence Hernando
Birth Date: December 15, 1973
Occupation: Physical Therapist
Experience: **Healed of a fever and cough**
Date of Testimony: July 16, 1999

I never knew how powerful spiritual strength was until I had a talk with Master Kim. Two weeks I was struggling with a bad cough and cold. I tried all kinds of medicine but nothing seemed to work. Master Kim noticed I was sick and he offered his help. By that time, I was running a very high fever; it was very difficult for me to breathe and speak. Master Kim offered me a different kind of help. He showed me a very powerful defense against sickness: the power of the Bible and the Word of the Lord. Through him I met Jesus Christ. Master Kim introduced me again to the power of faith in the Lord. He and I prayed together and my faith was strengthened. I was enlightened and reminded of the power I already have...the power of my faith in Jesus Christ, and His word in the Bible. I remind myself everyday that I have the power of my Lord through my faith.

#6: Elena Karimova
Birth Date: December 5, 1965
Occupation: Not Recorded
Experience: **Healed from mastopathy and back pain**
Date of Testimony: April 11, 2000

My name is Elena and I come from Russia. In my country, there wasn't any religion before the revolution happened. After the communists came, they claimed that God does not exist. They said religion is like cocaine to keep people under control by the rich. I heard these things from kindergarten through college. Something inside me told me that there was something wrong with that. I started to think about it seriously when an amazing transformation happened to my father who was so bad his entire life. He tried to quit smoking and drinking so many times, and he couldn't. One day he really believed in God, and he quit smoking and drinking. God healed him from the disease, which was almost killing him! What happened shocked me so much, but something was keeping me away from God. I know now that God always wanted me to be with Him.

I told Master Kim about all my problems and he said that God can solve all of them just in one moment. I had back pain, joint and neck problems, and I had mastopathy in my breasts. Master prayed for me very hard. The next day I woke up with no pain. I also had a mammogram that shows there are no problems anymore. Thank you, God!

#7: Roman Chekovsky
Birth Date: June 18, 1976
Occupation: Actuary
Experience: **Healed of insomnia**
Date of Testimony: June 14, 1999

I have had trouble sleeping for the past few months. As I work in a field that requires mental concentration, the little sleep that I was getting was affecting my performance. Even when I was physically and mentally tired, I just could not sleep. When I told Master DJ Kim about my problem, he said it was the demon inside of me that was not letting me sleep, so that I did not have enough energy to achieve my goals.

On June 4, 1999, Master DJ Kim prayed with me to Jesus Christ to cast out my demon. During prayer I felt a force inside of me that was resisting and started to have memories of bad things that happened in the past. As the praying continued, I also started to cry. Since that day, I have been sleeping well, and have more energy during the day.

#8: Richard Lupillo
Birth Date: July 14, 1956
Occupation: Chemist
Experience: **Healed from a knee injury**
Date of Testimony: November 23, 1999

On Friday 11/5/99, I got pain in my knee. I felt very bad, but I struggled and went to Tae Kwon Do. I never mentioned anything to Mr. Kim. Then the pain got worse. I finally told him and after I finished my class, I hardly could run or jump. I felt that my joint was worn out. After class, we prayed. He asked me, "Do you believe in Jesus?" I replied, "Yes I do." Then after he finished, I felt good, but as soon as I walked outside, the pain got bad on my knee again. The pain was so bad that I cried like a child. I went to the hospital and they gave me a needle (cortisone) and I took a painkiller too (Voltaire). I skipped class for a week until Friday. When I went back to class, Mr. Kim saw me in bad shape. Then he told me to never give up, and we prayed harder. After we prayed, I felt like a brand new man. I feel more strength and no more pain. Lord, thank you, I'm much better. Thank you, Jesus. I can do all things through Christ, which strengthens me. (Philippians 4:13)

#9: Shelly Stratano
Birth Date: August 22, 1978
Occupation: None
Experience: **Healed from sinus inflammation**
Date of Testimony: April 10, 1995

I believed in Jesus for a long time, but never really experienced his power for healing. Until one day I had a really bad headache and it was really affecting my performance and my attitude. I went to the doctor and he said it was a sinus inflammation. I was taking medicine but it didn't seem to help any. One day after Tae Kwon Do, I told Master Kim about it. He told me that Jesus was going to help me. All I had to do was believe in Him, which I did. Master Kim prayed for me. As he was praying, I felt like crying. My eyes were tearing. I felt shaky, but relieved. I felt like whatever was in my body was gone. When I got home I thanked Jesus for helping me. Ever since that day, my sinus hasn't bothered me at all. I feel newly refreshed-like someone was smiling on my soul that day. I can say that I have felt the power of Jesus and I believe He is with me. Now that I am healed, I want to thank Jesus.

#10: Lucy Gaftson
Birth Date: September 24, 1968
Occupation: Secretary
Experience: **Healed of lumps in her body**
Date of Testimony: October 19, 1993

About two years ago, around July 1990, I noticed small bumps under my armpits, groin area, and the back of my neck. They were about the size of marbles, very close to the back of my head. I started to think crazy and thought they were some kind of tumors. There were about 6 of them. I felt no pain or headaches or any symptoms at all. I never bothered to get them checked because I was afraid that they were cysts or tumors. I figured if they didn't hurt or bother me at all, to leave them alone. In October of 1993, my job was being terminated, and I was losing my insurance. I thought I would get these bumps checked out before losing the insurance. I was going for a biopsy, where they were to cut a small incision in my neck and test it. The day before that appointment, I called to find out my blood test results. To my surprise, it turned out that I was HIV positive. I nearly lost my mind. I went back the same day for another blood test that came back the same. I came to Master Kim crying hysterically and was petrified when I found this out. He had just spoken to me about God and Jesus Christ only two weeks before. On that same day, we prayed together for a couple of hours. I went home from that night and prayed and prayed. Four days later I noticed the swollen glands shrinking after being there over four years. On the fifth day, I went up to Master Kim and he asked if they were almost gone. He knew that Jesus is faithful to His word and was confident that the bumps were shrinking. The power of God is very strong. I was happy to have someone like Master Kim to explain the Bible to me. That was the only thing I had to keep me from losing my mind or trying to kill myself because of the devil.

#11: Gerald Manker
Birth Date: October 11, 1967
Occupation: Truck Driver
Experience: **Healed of encephalitis photogenic amnesia and a seizure disorder**
Date of Testimony: January 26, 1995

I got really sick on October 11, 1992. I had a fever of 104 degrees, extremely bad headaches and backaches. I was admitted into the hospital on October 12, 1992 and stayed there for over two weeks. I was diagnosed with encephalitis photogenic amnesia and a seizure disorder. I had at least 8 seizures between October 14, 1992 and October 28, 1994. The doctors told me I was not an epileptic, but I was suffering from seizures. I was very frustrated and angry. My wife told Master Kim about my disorder and he wanted to see me. My wife and I went to see Master Kim and spent about four hours with him. We read from the Bible and then prayed. Master Kim prayed for me and I prayed for myself. It has been four months and I have not had a seizure since. My family and I are so thankful that God healed me.

#12: Toni-Lee Sangastiano
Birth Date: September 12,1974
Occupation: College Student
Experience: **Healed of an ankle injury**
Date of Testimony: June 18, 1996

In May 1996, I hurt my ankle while trying to do some type of jumping kick my first week as a white belt at a Hapkido school in my town. After, I had a slight limp, and I could not even attempt to kneel back and sit on my feet without a searing pain in my left ankle.

Later that evening, I met Master Kim. Master Kim proceeded to ask if I believed in God while he moved my left foot around. "Y-Yes," I said, after I squirmed in my seat from the pain. Master Kim instructed a congested black belt and I to go and pray. As I sat on the floor praying for myself, I watched Master Kim cast out the demons through the use of the Bible. By the time Master Kim was done, this once congested black belt sounded perfectly normal. "Wow," I thought. Then it was my turn. I listened to Master Kim as he explained to me that it is God who is going to help me. He read passages from the Bible explaining when people get sick or hurt it is because there are demons inside of us. Those demons have to be cast out, or they will manifest themselves inside of us. From there, the demons work on us physically by causing illness or injury, proceeding to work on us mentally until they drag us further away from God. He also told me that I was lost and that I should be closer to God because I am young and easily influenced, because I wasn't as close to God as I should be.

After our talk, Master Kim had me read passages aloud in the Bible so I would understand why and what he was about to do. He repeatedly ordered the demons out of my body, telling them to leave me alone in the name of Jesus. When I let Master Kim move my left foot around, it didn't hurt!!! I was astonished! I then prayed to thank God. Before I left there that night, I was jumping around running without any problem!

#13: Steve Hannett
Birth Date: April 3, 1974
Occupation: College Student
Experience: **Healed from cancer**
Date of Testimony: March 20, 1994

On July 29, 1993, I learned that I had Hodgkin's disease—cancer of the lymph nodes. The doctors were unaware of what caused the cancer. Some doctors said stress, others said my environment. Ultimately, they told me they had no idea. I underwent radiation treatment of my chest and throat from September

7 through October 13. Needless to say, the treatment was unpleasant and caused side effects. There were damaged cells in my throat causing me to cough and making it difficult to walk even short distances. Eager to strengthen myself, I sought to study martial arts and met Master Kim. He showed me the power of prayer in Jesus Christ, and explained that the true cause of all sickness and disease is evil. Although it seemed foreign and strange at the time, I listened as Master Kim explained the truth of the Bible—basically that Jesus Christ died for us and cleaned all of our sin. He defeated evil and we are now free of all diseases, sorrow, and pain. Master Kim explained that this is God's promise to us and will never be broken.

On Friday, May 20, Master Kim laid his hands on my head and commanded the unclean spirit to leave me in the name of Jesus Christ. My body began to shake and the evil spirit that caused my cancer left. I immediately felt peaceful, and knew that everything the Bible teaches is true. We are healed by the stripes of Jesus Christ! I no longer had the cough or pain in my back... they were gone. After a doctor's examination I was found clear of cancer and there have been no signs of cancer at all. Contrary to what I used to believe, it isn't how strong your body is that matters. It is how strong your spirit is that really counts. Since May, I have continued to grow spiritually, and have been healed many times by Jesus Christ. I am no longer afraid of cancer or of any disease because I know that with faith anything is possible!

#14: Cathy Greene
Occupation: Post Office Clerk
Experience: **Healed from headache and sickness**
Date of Testimony: March 24, 1995

I have been a student of Master Kim's for six years. Throughout that time, I have seen him help his students in many ways. Most importantly, I have seen him pray with his students in the power of the name of Jesus Christ. I myself have been sick or injured on lots of occasions and he has helped me out. The last time was a few days ago 3-22-95. I had a very bad cold and was feeling very dizzy, so dizzy that I could not move without feeling very lightheaded. I called Master Kim and went over to the school. When I got there, he told me to read a passage from the Bible but I could hardly see the page. I felt so bad. A few minutes later we prayed together and then he prayed over me. I could feel my head hurting for a few minutes, and I was very warm and felt very tired and drained, but I also felt the dizzy headaches were going. By the time Master Kim was finished praying over me, my head had stopped hurting and all the dizziness was gone. I felt so tired and drained, but really felt so much better. Years ago people believed that the laying on of hands and the power of prayer could heal the body and soul, and that the power of belief in God could overcome great odds. This is still true today. With more belief in prayer and God, things can be changed. Master Kim lives by that way and has helped many people who have lost their way in life and have felt sickness and pain. Have an open heart and mind, believe in God, and prayer can do great things. All you have to do is try.

#15: Melissa Alban
Birth Date: July 17, 1976
Occupation: Student
Experience: **Healed of chronic headaches**
Date of Testimony: March 27, 1995

I was having really bad headaches. They were getting so bad that I couldn't do anything about them, aspirin didn't even help. These headaches were going on for about a year or so. My brother is a student and encouraged me to meet Master Kim. I met Master Kim because I was leaving for college for the first time and couldn't go away with this problem. He helped me see and learn what was going on in me. He had me read passages in the Bible, passages I've never read before. He opened my eyes more to God and Jesus. After this, he began praying. I prayed and as he laid his hands on my head, this tremendous overwhelming feeling came over me. I became exhausted and it took a lot out of me. When it was over I felt refreshed, empty, clear-headed and just renewed actually, like a weight being lifted from me. After this experience, my headaches went away. I find myself turning to God more. The full experience is really hard to explain because it was very different from anything I've ever experienced. It was something I feel is good to experience as a person especially at my young age because it opened my eyes and cleaned my mind to let God in and for Him to help me. Overall, I feel free from problems and I know if ever there is a problem, that God can get me through it and that any pain or sickness can be released through the laying on of hands and faith. I've always thought of it as a joke, making fun of TV evangelists, but it's not. It's true, and taking it seriously is a must. It was an experience I can never forget.

#16: Scott Redmana
Birth Date: April 5, 1953
Occupation: Sales
Experience: **Healed from bursitis in hip**
Date of Testimony: February 14, 1997

For months I had a very discomforting pain in my right hip. It came very suddenly and with no explanation. I am an avid golfer and thought it was caused by a certain turn in my swing. After three months of hoping that it would pass on its own, I finally sought the help of my doctor. By just showing him where the pain was, he automatically diagnosed it as bursitis, and told me to take Tylenol three times a day. When I asked, do I have to do this every day of my life, he said only when it acts up. Low and behold it *did not* work. One day, when attending one of my son's classes at The Blue Dragon Karate School, his teacher, Master Kim, asked how I was feeling. I began to tell him about my hip problem. He began telling me how many people he has helped in the past through spiritual healing and prayer. Well for many weeks of doubt and speculation and running out of tolerance of the pain that was continuing to inflict me, I decided to make an appointment with Master Kim.

Master Kim talked to me a little and made me feel very comfortable on what was about to take place. We prayed together and asked God to help me. He then laid his hands on the front of my head and proceeded to pray very strongly to release any pain that I was experiencing. We prayed for more than an hour. I am amazed that to this day, two months after that pain has never returned to me. I'm very grateful and most of all a believer in prayer and spiritual healing. May God bless all who read this.

#17: Sarah Trellis
Birth Date: May 1, 1951
Occupation: Teacher
Experience: **Healed of a shoulder, back, and neck injuries**
Date of Testimony: September 20, 1997

On June 12, 1997, I was slammed backwards into a locker in the hallway during a fight. I was talking to a boy that a gang was after and someone grabbed me by my right shoulder (from behind) and slammed me out of the way. I hurt my neck, right shoulder, and lower center back. I suffered muscle spasms, severe neck and shoulder pain, and numbness with shooting pains in the head, neck, and arm. I had therapy for my neck, shoulder, and back all summer. I took painkillers and muscle relaxers to no avail.

My son attends Master Kim's school and Master Kim offered to help. Master Kim reviewed scripture with me and prayed with me. I was amazed at the simplicity of the concept of spiritual healing. I had seen the very same scripture many times before, but I did not understand until Master Kim explained it to me. After the healing and praying, I felt weak at first, but very peaceful and relaxed. My neck, back, and shoulders all felt fine. My spirit had been repaired, and my body felt free, relaxed, and pain free!

#18: Vincent Molinaro, Jr.
Birth Date: August 10, 1960
Occupation: Truck Driver
Experience: **Healed of drug addiction, nosebleeds, knee injury, and mother-in-law healed of cancer**
Date of Testimony: March 30, 1995

As a teenager, I was involved in drugs, sex, and worshiped the devil. Six years ago, I met my wife, Lisa, who helped me to get help. So I went into rehabilitation for 38 days, and when I was finished, I started to go to AA where I found God. It was good, but not enough. One day on the job I met a friend who was a born-again Christian. He told me that Jesus would be able to save my life. So I made a confession that Jesus was my Lord and that He died for my sins.

When I first started Tae Kwon Do, I was having a lot of trouble with my nose from all the drugs, so I spoke to Master Kim and he told me that he would be able to fix it with the power of Jesus. So Master Kim cast out a demon.

I also had a very bad time when my wife was having our baby. The X-rays said that the baby was going to be deformed. I was very upset and lost my faith. So again I was at school and Master Kim asked what was wrong. So I told Master Kim and he was very concerned. After class we got together and prayed. Master Kim again cast out a very powerful demon who was sent by Satan to destroy my baby and my wife. This all took place in 1994. The demon would not come out, but Master Kim did not give up. He cast the demon out in Jesus' name, but Satan did not give up. When Jessica, my daughter, was born she was very sick and almost didn't make it. Lisa and myself prayed very hard for Jesus to help us once again. To make a long story short, Jessica is a miracle baby. Today she is 13 months old and doing great, so once again the power of Jesus is great.

In January of 1995, I was at work and had a great pain in my knee. I could not stand so I went to the hospital and the X-ray said that I would need surgery. So this went on for a couple of weeks and the knee was not getting better. Once again I went to Master Kim and he laid hands on me and cast out a demon. After a few weeks, the knee was not getting better so I went before the pastor and elders of my church and they prayed over me and anointed my knee with oil. It felt better for awhile but still not perfect. So one night I spoke with Master Kim and he said I didn't understand! We cast out a demon, we prayed, plus I went to church. So he told me that the problem was not the Lord, it was me. I lost faith and was not letting the Lord help me. So I went home and prayed, and in a week my knee was better.

A few months ago my mother-in-law had cancer and it didn't look good, so I prayed very hard and asked the Lord to heal her. Once again, the power of prayer is great. She went into surgery and came out in flying colors. The doctor could not believe that the cancer was gone. My life is so much better with Jesus in it.

––––––––––

19: Greg Lupeco
Birth Date: January 14, 1953
Occupation: Fork Lift Operator
Experience: **Healed of many medical problems**
Date of Testimony: November 24, 2001

I've had many medical problems where the evil one got inside me and caused me much pain and discomfort. Talking to the Lord by prayer and casting out the evil in the name of Jesus has made me better. I'm telling you, each time the pain left and I felt fine. It's almost unbelievable. You think you can't see the Lord or hear Him, but you can. As your faith gets stronger, the message gets louder and clearer. What the Lord has done for me is a miracle. That's the truth. He saved my life and I'm saved. I love life and the Lord is the one responsible for this. Grace, mercy and peace from God the Father and Christ Jesus our Lord. Amen.

About Conquerors In Christ
World Ministries

Conquerors In Christ World Ministries, Inc. is an international teaching and praying ministry whose goal is to bring glory to the name of Jesus Christ by supplying the physical and spiritual needs of a lost and hurting world. Following is our three-fold mission:

Save the Lost: To teach the entire and unadulterated truth of Jesus Christ to the entire world relying solely on the Holy Bible as the source of infallible teaching and guidance. The primary focus of this mission is to teach people how to become partakers of God's grace through the atoning sacrifice of Jesus Christ to receive the forgiveness of sin and the gift of eternal life.

Free the Oppressed: To teach people how to stand on the promises of God, and to pray with people to overcome every type of oppression whether physical, mental, or spiritual.

Equip the Saved: To help develop, train, and stand with Christians enabling them to grow in the grace and knowledge of Jesus Christ to maximize the glory brought to the name of Jesus Christ.

Please visit us at www.conquerorsinchrist.org **to learn more about how you can become a partner of Conquerors In Christ World Ministries!**

Note from the Authors

This book testifies to the power of God and the sure promises contained in the Bible. These truths have proven themselves true time and time again over centuries of scrupulous study and investigation. The word of the Lord Jesus Christ is faithful and sure in its accuracy as God confirms His word with many accompanying signs. (Mark 16:20) Given this fact, it is our desire for each individual to wholly and diligently seek the face of God as they persevere deeper into a greater faith where they can testify of God's power and walk in His promises free from all sickness, disease, and weakness. Please note, however, that the authors are in no way, shape, or form offering medical advice or making recommendations to individuals whether or not to seek or continue to seek medical attention for various maladies. This decision is left solely to an individual based on their faith, experience, and personal preference. The authors, therefore, hold themselves harmless from any and all losses, damages, and liabilities resulting from an individual's specific decisions regarding the treatment of their problems.